THE PRACTITIONER IN

Marilyn Cochran-Smith and Susan L. Lytle, Series Editors

Professional Development in Relational Learning Communities: Teachers in Connection
Miriam B. Raider-Roth

Impactful Practitioner Inquiry: The Ripple Effect on Classrooms, Schools, and Teacher Professionalism
Sue Nichols & Phil Cormack

Teaching in Themes:
An Approach to Schoolwide Learning, Creating Community, and Differentiating Instruction
Deborah Meier, Matthew Knoester, & Katherine Clunis D'Andrea, Eds.

Family Dialogue Journals: School–Home Partnerships That Support Student Learning
JoBeth Allen, Jennifer Beaty, Angela Dean, Joseph Jones, Stephanie Smith Mathews, Jen McCreight, Elyse Schwedler, & Amber M. Simmons

Raising Race Questions:
Whiteness and Inquiry in Education
Ali Michael

Making Space for Active Learning:
The Art and Practice of Teaching
Anne C. Martin & Ellen Schwartz, Eds.

The First Year of Teaching:
Classroom Research to Increase Student Learning
Jabari Mahiri & Sarah Warshauer Freedman, Eds.

A Critical Inquiry Framework for K–12 Teachers:
Lessons and Resources from the U.N. Rights of the Child
JoBeth Allen & Lois Alexander, Eds.

Democratic Education in Practice:
Inside the Mission Hill School
Matthew Knoester

Action Research in Special Education: An Inquiry Approach for Effective Teaching and Learning
Susan M. Bruce & Gerald J. Pine

Inviting Families into the Classroom:
Learning from a Life in Teaching
Lynne Yermanock Strieb

Jenny's Story: Taking the Long View of the Child —Prospect's Philosophy in Action
Patricia F. Carini & Margaret Himley, with Carol Christine, Cecilia Espinosa, & Julia Fournier

Acting Out! Combating Homophobia Through Teacher Activism
Mollie V. Blackburn, Caroline T. Clark, Lauren M. Kenney, & Jill M. Smith, Eds.

Puzzling Moments, Teachable Moments: Practicing Teacher Research in Urban Classrooms
Cynthia Ballenger

Inquiry as Stance:
Practitioner Research for the Next Generation
Marilyn Cochran-Smith & Susan L. Lytle

Building Racial and Cultural Competence in the Classroom: Strategies from Urban Educators
Karen Manheim Teel & Jennifer Obidah, Eds.

Re-Reading Families: The Literate Lives of Urban Children, Four Years Later
Catherine Compton-Lilly

"What About Rose?" Using Teacher Research to Reverse School Failure
Smokey Wilson

Immigrant Students and Literacy:
Reading, Writing, and Remembering
Gerald Campano

Going Public with Our Teaching:
An Anthology of Practice
Thomas Hatch, Dilruba Ahmed, Ann Lieberman, Deborah Faigenbaum, Melissa Eiler White, & Désirée H. Pointer Mace, Eds.

Teaching as Inquiry: Asking Hard Questions to Improve Practice and Student Achievement
Alexandra Weinbaum, David Allen, Tina Blythe, Katherine Simon, Steve Seidel, & Catherine Rubin

"Is This English?" Race, Language, and Culture in the Classroom
Bob Fecho

Teacher Research for Better Schools
Marian M. Mohr, Courtney Rogers, Betsy Sanford, Mary Ann Nocerino, Marion S. MacLean, & Sheila Clawson

Imagination and Literacy:
A Teacher's Search for the Heart of Learning
Karen Gallas

(continued)

PRACTITIONER INQUIRY SERIES, *continued*

Regarding Children's Words:
Teacher Research on Language and Literacy
BROOKLINE TEACHER RESEARCHER SEMINAR

Rural Voices: Place-Conscious Education and the Teaching of Writing
ROBERT E. BROOKE, ED.

Teaching Through the Storm: A Journal of Hope
KAREN HALE HANKINS

Reading Families:
The Literate Lives of Urban Children
CATHERINE COMPTON-LILLY

Narrative Inquiry in Practice:
Advancing the Knowledge of Teaching
NONA LYONS & VICKI KUBLER LABOSKEY, EDS.

Starting Strong: A Different Look at Children, Schools, and Standards
PATRICIA F. CARINI

Because of the Kids: Facing Racial and Cultural Differences in Schools
JENNIFER E. OBIDAH & KAREN MANHEIM TEEL

Ethical Issues in Practitioner Research
JANE ZENI, ED.

Action, Talk, and Text:
Learning and Teaching Through Inquiry
GORDON WELLS, ED.

Teaching Mathematics to the New Standards:
Relearning the Dance
RUTH M. HEATON

Teacher Narrative as Critical Inquiry:
Rewriting the Script
JOY S. RITCHIE & DAVID E. WILSON

From Another Angle:
Children's Strengths and School Standards
MARGARET HIMLEY WITH PATRICIA F. CARINI, EDS.

Inside City Schools: Investigating
Literacy in the Multicultural Classroom
SARAH WARSHAUER FREEDMAN, ELIZABETH RADIN SIMONS, JULIE SHALHOPE KALNIN, ALEX CASARENO, & THE M-CLASS TEAMS

Class Actions: Teaching for Social Justice in Elementary and Middle School
JOBETH ALLEN, ED.

Teacher/Mentor:
A Dialogue for Collaborative Learning
PEG GRAHAM, SALLY HUDSON-ROSS, CHANDRA ADKINS, PATTI MCWHORTER, & JENNIFER MCDUFFIE STEWART, EDS.

Teaching Other People's Children: Literacy and Learning in a Bilingual Classroom
CYNTHIA BALLENGER

Teaching, Multimedia, and Mathematics:
Investigations of Real Practice
MAGDALENE LAMPERT & DEBORAH LOEWENBERG BALL

John Dewey and the Challenge of
Classroom Practice
STEPHEN M. FISHMAN & LUCILLE MCCARTHY

"Sometimes I Can Be Anything":
Power, Gender, and Identity in a Primary Classroom
KAREN GALLAS

Learning in Small Moments:
Life in an Urban Classroom
DANIEL R. MEIER

Professional Development in Relational Learning Communities

Teachers in Connection

Miriam B. Raider-Roth

Foreword by Sharon Feiman-Nemser

TEACHERS COLLEGE PRESS

TEACHERS COLLEGE | COLUMBIA UNIVERSITY

NEW YORK AND LONDON

Published by Teachers College Press, 1234 Amsterdam Avenue, New York, NY 10027

Cover photo by Harvey S. Tillis.

Library of Congress Cataloging-in-Publication Data

Names: Raider-Roth, Miriam B.
Title: Professional development in relational learning communities : teachers in connection / Miriam B. Raider-Roth ; foreword by Sharon Feiman-Nemser.
Description: New York : Teachers College Press, 2017. | Series: Practitioner inquiry series | Includes bibliographical references and index.
Identifiers: LCCN 2016048512 (print) | LCCN 2016049254 (ebook)
ISBN 9780807758151 (pbk. : alk. paper)
ISBN 9780807758168 (hardcover : alk. paper)
ISBN 9780807775578 (ebook)
Subjects: LCSH: Teachers—Professional relationships. | Professional learning communities. | Teachers—Training of.
Classification: LCC LB1775 .R235 2017 (print) | LCC LB1775 (ebook) | DDC 371.1—dc23
LC record available at https://lccn.loc.gov/2016048512

ISBN 978-0-8077-5815-1 (paper)
ISBN 978-0-8077-5816-8 (hardcover)
ISBN 978-0-8077-7557-8 (ebook)

Printed on acid-free paper
Manufactured in the United States of America

24 23 22 21 20 19 18 17 8 7 6 5 4 3 2 1

To my parents, Chaya and Walter Roth,
my first and enduring teachers

Contents

Foreword

I first met Miriam Raider-Roth in the 1990s at an annual meeting of the North Dakota Study Group on Evaluation (NDSG), a network of progressive educators deeply committed to excellence and equity in public education. At the time, Raider-Roth was a doctoral student at the Graduate School of Education at Harvard; her mentor, the late Vito Perrone, founder and convener of the NDSG, brought her to the meeting and introduced us. What began as a mentoring relationship evolved into a personal and professional friendship based on our mutual interests in teacher learning, democratic schooling, and Jewish education. Over the years I learned a lot from Miriam Raider-Roth about relational psychology and its application to studies of teaching and learning. In this book, she brings this understanding to a new level of conceptual and practical sophistication by elaborating a relational model of professional development and connecting it to a set of powerful pedagogies.

The book grows out of a decade-long action research project carried out in the context of three summer seminars for teachers sponsored by the Center for the Study of Jewish Culture and Education at the University of Cincinnati. Each of the seminars, which lasted 5 days, included a diverse group of educators from public, private, and parochial schools and, during one seminar, a group of rabbinical students from a local college. Participants were responsible for teaching world religions and culture in their social studies, language arts, and/or Jewish studies classes. On the premise that learning about one culture can create a bridge for understanding diverse cultures, the seminars focused on the teaching and learning of Jewish history and culture. Across the seminars, Raider-Roth and the other leaders, along with a group of doctoral students, studied their practice as facilitators of "culturally focused professional development" and the participants' learning.

Raider-Roth's book invites several different readings, each well developed in theory and practice. It can be read as a portrait of a "relational learning community in action." It can be read as a toolkit for teacher educators and professional developers. It can be read as an account of deep, transformative teacher learning. It can be read as a powerful example of practitioner research into professional development. Together these readings make a compelling argument for the creation of trusting learning environments where teachers explore cultural differences and develop capacities for democratic teaching.

David Hawkins' (1974/2002) classic essay, "I, Thou, It," provides the conceptual foundation for Raider-Roth's "relational learning community" (RLC) model. Hawkins argues that the relationship between teacher and students differs from other close relationships because of the presence of a third element, the subject matter ("it"), which provides a shared focus for inquiry. Other scholars have situated the teacher/learner/subject matter triangle within a circle to represent the multiple layers of context that shape and are shaped by the other three elements. Raider-Roth calls it a "relational triangle" to highlight the interdependence of teacher, learners, subject matter, and the environment.

In the RLC described in this book, the seminar facilitators are the teachers, the educators are the learners, the subject matter is the history, religion, and culture of the American Jewish community, and the context is the "holding environment" that the seminar leaders carefully constructed and nurtured. As a model of professional development, the RLC builds on a growing body of scholarship on teacher learning in community, but it pays special attention to the relational dynamics in which the learning takes place and to the identity challenges that the study of culture in a diverse group can evoke.

One unique feature of the book is the detailed descriptions of the seminar's core pedagogies and their associated practices. Raider-Roth discusses three pedagogies, all of which involve close study of texts, broadly defined. The seminar immersed participants in a traditional mode of Jewish text study called *hevruta*. Participants studied short Talmudic texts in pairs, experimenting with the interpretive practices of voicing, supporting, and challenging. They engaged in disciplined observations of texts, suspending judgment in order to open up new possibilities of seeing. They investigated a variety of historical "texts," including archival documents, paintings, films, and physical spaces, using a specific approach to historiographic inquiry. Raider-Roth calls these "relational cultural pedagogies" because they depend on "being present" to self, text, and other and they create opportunities to wrestle with cultural differences.

Raider-Roth invites us into the thinking of the seminar leaders as they work to create an environment where it is legitimate to disagree, challenge, and leave one's comfort zone. We learn what goes into facilitating productive, growth producing conversations and learning opportunities. We also hear how participants experience these opportunities and how they influence their perspectives and understandings. The voices of participants permeate the book as they confront their own and their partners' cultural assumptions and reflect on their identities as learners and teachers. This is especially true for moments of disequilibrium when participants experience challenges to their personal, professional, and cultural identities.

The focus on participants' learning both during and after the seminar is a real strength of the book. Raider-Roth documents shifts in participants' thinking and self-understanding in response to the seminar's content, pedagogy, and environment. The evidence, based on reflective writing and interviews, leaves a strong impression that the seminar was a transformative experience for many. One particularly moving account comes from a participant who explains how the seminar helped her knock down an "internal wall. . . . the wall of segregation, the wall of ignorance, the wall of judgments, the wall of not understanding" (pp. 112–113). As Raider-Roth points out, such deep learning depends not only on a diverse learning community, but also on relational supports that allow for the release of old ideas and the construction of new ones.

The book also offers a rare example of practitioner inquiry in the context of professional development. The main research question concerns the nature of participants' learning both during and after the seminar and the ways in which different aspects of the seminar contribute to that learning. Here too the research methods are relational. Researchers not only positioned themselves as partners in learning during the seminar, they also attended to the relational dynamics within the research group itself. For interested readers, Appendix B provides an overview of practitioner inquiry and a detailed discussion of the research methods for each phase of this action research project that produced both theoretical and practical knowledge about professional development.

Professional Development in Relational Communities is an especially timely book. It offers a serious model of professional development that fosters deep learning about self and other. It demonstrates that living new approaches to teaching historical and cultural texts can increase the likelihood that educators will bring these practices home to their classrooms. It makes the case that attending to relational dynamics is key to promoting transformative learning for teachers and their students. It speaks to some of the most pressing educational challenges of our time—how to combat racism and ignorance and cultivate the habits of mind and heart necessary for democracy to function.

—Sharon Feiman-Nemser

Acknowledgments

This book would not have been possible without the multiple collaborations that were the fabric of the work on which it is based. First and foremost, I want to thank all of the teachers who participated in the summer seminars, who agreed to participate in the action research studies, and who gave generously of their time, spirit, and wisdom. You have accompanied me every step of the writing of this book.

To the teachers and facilitators of the summer seminars, Mark A. Raider, Elie Holzer, Haim Rechnitzer, Richard Sarason, Vicki Stieha, and Mark Kohan, I am deeply grateful for your collaboration, creativity, intellectual inspiration, and hours of discussion about teaching and learning. The work that happened in the seminars and in this book was only possible because of the work of Mark A. Raider, my husband, professional partner, and co-founder of the Center for Studies in Jewish Education and Culture (CSJEC) at the University of Cincinnati. As the co-creator of the concept and enactor of the seminars, Mark was core to creating the vision of the Center and the professional development work that has been central to the Center's mission.

To the action research team, Vicki Stieha, Billy Hensley, Mark Kohan, and Carrie Turpin, who worked tirelessly and collaboratively with great curiosity, intellectual rigor, and joyful humor, many many thanks. Our relational learning communities were always the highlights of my week! Vicki was core to each and every cycle of action research, gently supporting and challenging the emerging ideas, questions, and findings. Many thanks to Vicki and Mark for conducting relationally sensitive and inquiring interviews.

I owe a great debt of gratitude to the Jacob Rader Marcus Center of the American Jewish Archives on the Cincinnati campus of the Hebrew Union College–Jewish Institute of Religion for hosting the summer seminars and providing essential resources, including beautiful space, unparalleled archival resources, and logistical support. Heartfelt thanks to Dr. Gary P. Zola, Lisa Frankel, Al Simandl, Kevin Proffitt, and Dana Herman.

The summer seminars were generously funded by the Jewish Foundation of Cincinnati; the Jewish Federation of Cincinnati; the Ohio Humanities Council; the Dean's Office of the College of Education, Human Services, and Criminal Justice at the University of Cincinnati; and the Posen

Foundation, U.S. For our 2010 seminar, Cincinnati Shakespeare Company graciously hosted a staged reading of David Ives' play *New Jerusalem, The Interrogation of Baruch de Spinoza at Talmud Torah Congregation: Amsterdam, July 27, 1656*. Many thanks to Ari Roth for introducing the play to us and expertly directing its staged reading and to the Cincy Shakes ensemble for their talented performance.

Our seminars were enriched and supported by Sharon Feiman-Nemser, founding director of the Mandel Center for Studies in Jewish Education at Brandeis University. Sharon has offered warm mentorship from the creation of CSJEC to the present, and has generously shared her time, resources, and wisdom.

I am grateful to the faculty of the Mandel Teacher Educator Institute (MTEI)—Gail Dorph, Seymour Kopelowitz, Sharon Feiman-Nemser, Barry Holtz, Elie Holzer, Jennifer Lewis, and Kathy Simon—who embraced the ideas in this book, supported and challenged my thinking, and offered me the opportunity to try out the findings in my teaching at MTEI. Heartfelt gratitude to the members of Cohort 7, who offered honest and helpful feedback to the big ideas I shared.

I deeply appreciate Susan Lytle and Marilyn Cochran-Smith, editors of Teachers College Press' Practitioner Inquiry Series, for including this volume in this collection of publications. It is a true honor to be included in such an illustrious group of authors. The book would not have come to light without the steadfast encouragement of Susan Lytle: Her belief in the ideas and methodology supported my capacity to write. Many thanks to Brian Ellerbeck, Sarah Biondello, and Karl Nyberg for their editorial support and shepherding this project to completion.

The first drafts of this book were written during my sabbatical from the University of Cincinnati, and I am grateful to Dr. Mary Boat and the School of Education for supporting this academic leave to pursue my writing. Many thanks to Mary Brydon-Miller, Susan Lytle, and Carol Rodgers, who generously read drafts of the book, and offered insightful and essential feedback. You formed an interpretative community to help me hear the dimensions of my own voice. Heartfelt thanks to Amy Rector Aranda, for her editorial support in reading drafts of the book, creating and improving the quality of the figures, and her expert research assistance.

My mentors Carol Gilligan and Harriet Cuffaro (1928–2016) inspire every page of this volume. Beginning in 1994, Carol has taught me the foundations of relational theory and the interconnections with research, teaching, learning, and democracy. I continue to learn from her to this day. Harriet Cuffaro was a steadfast teacher, mentor, and friend from the moment I met her in 1987. My understandings of progressive education and John Dewey ("our friend John," as she liked to say) and my identity as a teacher are rooted in Harriet's teaching, writing, and mentorship. Harriet passed away during the writing of this book, but our many Japanese dinner conversations about Dewey and democracy deeply informed this book and especially Chapter 1. I dedicate this chapter to her. Harriet's memory is a profound blessing.

Mary Brydon-Miller and Lisa Vaughn, my cider sisters, have offered professional mentorship and personal light over the past decade. Our collective and joyful work in the University of Cincinnati Action Research Center has helped me understand and claim my identity as an action researcher. To Michelle Ernst, Orit Netter, Anna Rosen, Claire Rechnitzer, and Laura Wright, your steadfast friendship has provided safe harbor for me time and time again. To Mindy Nagel and Claudia Wright, thank you for your attentive care for my body and spirit throughout the writing of this book.

I am so fortunate to be embraced by a loving extended family. My parents, Chaya and Walter Roth, have consistently believed in my work, in the importance of writing, and in the meaning of making work public. Their own legacy as scholars and writers is a beacon of inspiration. My parents-in-law, Liz and David Raider, have been steadfast in their support and love for me as a daughter, and are role models in their commitment to community and family. To my siblings Judy Roth and Ari Roth, and my siblings-in-law Lani Raider, Daniel and Shari Raider, Kate Schecter, and Stephen P. Zeldes, you inspire me with your activism, creativity, commitment to justice, psychological and physical health, and your dedication to practice, the arts, and scholarship. My nieces and nephews, Isabel and Sophie Roth, Miko and Tema Zeldes-Roth, Elias and Yael Raider, are outstanding people who bring immense joy to our lives.

To Jonah, Ez, and Talia, I admire your quest for creativity, your courage in speaking your truths, and I love you with all my heart. Thank you for your patience with me as I wrote this book, for your supportive queries of "how's the book going?," and cheering me on as I hit the "send" button.

Finally, to Mark, because of your love, trust, and belief in me, I have been able to write and finish this book. Thank you for standing with me every step of the way, reading drafts as many times as I needed you to, and asking me to say more. You are my best friend, partner, and beloved.

—Miriam B. Raider-Roth, November 2016, Cincinnati, Ohio

Teachers in Connection

We live in an era in which the definition of *teacher* is in full-scale crisis. The conception of teacher has drifted toward that of "educational clerk," purveyor of skills, and one who does not make decisions about the content and pedagogy in the classroom but delivers that which others—often remote political officials and academic "experts"—deem important (Kumashiro, 2010; Sleeter, 2008; Zeichner, 2010). In addition to creating a technical professional, rather than a thoughtful, reflective, and intellectual one, teachers in this setting have little use for what they know. As they enact curriculum devised by others and implement mandated products, what happens to the "wonderful ideas" (Duckworth, 2006) that they construct in response to what they see happening in their classroom? Teachers risk "not knowing what they know" in order to comply with the mandates and scripts assigned to them to perform. In such a context, agency and voice are eroded. Building on the work of Apple (1996) and Sachs (2003), Zeichner (2010) argues for the importance of "democratic professionalism," which emphasizes "collaborative and cooperative action" as an essential response to a growing technocratic view of the teaching professional.

Current trends in professional development, however, do not mirror democratic professionalism. Teachers' success is measured by how much they raise students' test scores, rather than how much they refine and improve their practice (Sleeter, 2014). Despite a solid trajectory of research demonstrating that transformative professional development requires sustained, deep, local, and actively oriented learning (Darling-Hammond, Wei, Andree, Richardson, & Orphanos, 2009; Dorph, 2011; Guskey, 2002), we have witnessed a retreat from such collaborative models (Wei, Darling-Hammond, & Adamson, 2010). Instead, we see an increase in professional development that is focused on "'product implementation' aligned with standards and standardized tests" (Zeichner, 2010, p. 1546). Resources that once supported collaborative teacher study are disappearing from the landscape of professional development (Randi & Zeichner, 2004).

RELATIONAL LEARNING COMMUNITIES

This volume argues for the need for models of professional development that nurture a democratic, relational, and connected form of teaching. Lasting and transformative teacher learning can occur in the context of relational learning communities (RLCs)—teacher learning groups in which explicit attention is paid to the construction and nurturing of relationships between and among the participants, facilitators, texts/content, and context (Raider-Roth, Stieha, Kohan, & Turpin, 2014). Within the context of trustworthy relationships, teachers can reconnect with all that they know about teaching, learning, and their own identities (Gilligan, 1996; Raider-Roth, 2005a). They are then able to act on what they know in the best interest of their students. Such action allows teachers to cultivate their voices to participate in democratic life and model such action for their students.

The concept of RLCs is informed by and builds on research examining the place of collective and collegial forms of teacher professional learning. These groups are often referred to as communities of practice (Wenger, 1998), professional learning communities (PLCs), professional communities (Little, 2006), study groups (Hollins, McIntyle, DeBose, Hollins, & Towner, 2004), and teacher learning groups (TLGs) (Allen, 2013). The RLC model is also informed by those scholars investigating the nature of transformative professional development in collective settings (Cochran-Smith & Lytle, 2009; Kegan & Lahey, 2009; Mezirow, 2012; Miranda, 2012; Whitcomb, Borko, & Liston, 2009). The necessity of collective learning has been shown to be especially important for professional development (PD) that focuses on questions of diversity, culture, and identity because the relational needs and dynamics here are even more significant than in other PD settings (Jurow, 2009). When PD supports teachers' understandings of diverse cultures, matters of identity (theirs and their students') become a central dimension of the learning experience (Beijaard, Verloop, & Vermunt, 2000; Rodgers & Scott; 2008). As teachers examine their cultural assumptions, as well as their own personal and professional identities, they can experience feelings of vulnerability and empowerment (Miranda, 2012). Such emotions can derail the learning process if learners are not supported by processes and colleagues that can build a bridge to new learning. An RLC can provide a "holding environment" (Winnicott, 1960, Kegan, 1994)—a space in which risks can be taken and collegial support shared—that offers participants "an evolutionary bridge, a context for crossing over" to construct new knowledge (Kegan, 1994, p. 43).

What distinguishes the RLC from these other frameworks is its explicit attention to the creation of, maintenance of, and reflection on the functioning of relationships, understanding that the quality of learning is only as strong as the relationships in which the learning is constructed

(Raider-Roth, 2005a). In addition, RLCs attend to the identity challenges that can be evoked by subject matter, such as the study of culture.

This kind of work is profoundly both psychological and intellectual, as well as deeply contextual. In making connections to self, others, and content and context, aspects of personal, professional, and cultural identities are often confronted. These identity confrontations can be especially charged in the current depersonalized and disconnected culture of teaching. In reconnecting with knowledge about self, others, and the contexts in which they live—that may have been "shelved" or walled off (because of the inability to act on such knowledge)—teachers can experience myriad emotions. The intensity of experience can even lead to a "shutting down" of the learning process (Raider-Roth, Stieha, & Hensley, 2012). Thus, teacher educators must be alert to, and skilled in, facilitating RLCs to maximize connections, identify ruptures, and construct opportunities for repair that help participants understand the differences and tension that may have led to a break in relationship. Such moments of repair are crucial learning moments.

A critical dimension of RLCs is that of content, or the focal subject area for which an RLC was created. An important dimension of the place of the content/subject matter in professional development is that of understanding the relationship between *what* and *how* subject matter is being studied (Shulman & Sherin, 2007; Van Driel & Berry, 2012). Indeed, Grossman, Wineberg, and Woolworth (2001) identify this dual focus of studying content knowledge and the associated pedagogies as "an essential tension of teacher community" (p. 951). Taking this tension seriously means understanding the dynamics of relationship in adult learning that can sustain the construction of enduring knowledge of self, others, and content.

A core educational theory underlying the discussion that follows stems from David Hawkins's triangular model of the essential relationships in teaching and learning. In his landmark essay, "I, Thou, and It," Hawkins (1974/2002) argues that the relationships among teachers, students, and subject matter create a unique form of relationship that is different from friendship or familial ones. He argues that there is a deep and abiding interdependence among teacher, learner, and subject matter—or the I, Thou, and It. Each dyad in this triangle is informed and shaped by the other dyads. The third learning partner of the "it" is what distinguishes this relational dynamic from other types of relationships. Many scholars have built on Hawkins's work to add the circle of "context" around the triangle, highlighting the importance of the context or environment in which these learning relationships exist (e.g., Ball & Forzani, 2007; Raider-Roth, 2005a; Rodgers, 2002; Rodgers & Raider-Roth, 2006; see Figure I.1). While some refer to this triangular model as the "instructional triangle," my colleagues and I have given it a new name—"the relational triangle"—to highlight the centrality of the dynamics of relationship that occur within and around the triangle and its

Figure I.1. The Relational Triangle

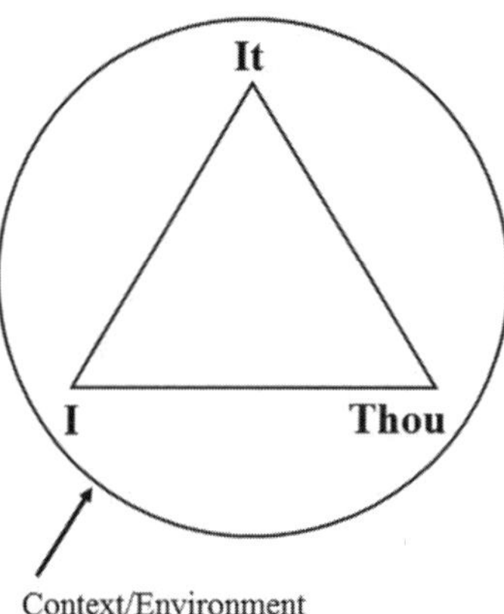

context. This model helps us understand the way the content/subject matter/texts mediate the relationships in an RLC.

Through a process of association and connection to self, others, and texts, RLCs can rekindle a vision of teaching that is agentic—where change is envisioned and acted upon. This requires being able to ask the questions "What needs to change in my classroom, school, and community?" and "How can my teaching help make this happen?" This is a vision of the teacher as a creator of social change (Counts, 1932/1978). Such a process of connection and association can undermine the disconnecting and depersonalizing forces being exerted in the arena of schooling today. This volume seeks to contribute to the educational landscape by making a case for such a vision of teaching.

TEACHING AND LEARNING ABOUT CULTURE

One domain in which teaching for social change is paramount is in the teaching and learning of culture. As Geneva Gay (2000) argues, "Culture is at the heart of all we do in education, whether that is curriculum, instruction, administration, or performance assessment" (p. 8). Building on Delgado-Gaitan and Trueba's (1991) work, she defines culture as "a dynamic system of social values, cultural codes, behavioral standards, worldviews, and beliefs used to give order and meaning to our own lives as well as the lives of others" (p. 8). This definition and understanding of culture and education provides a useful frame for this volume.

Teaching about culture in schools is delicate and necessary work in order to construct deeper, more nuanced knowledge and build stronger ties between students and teachers from diverse walks of life. Such teaching requires in-depth learning. RLCs are particularly important in professional development opportunities that focus on the study of culture. This kind of inquiry often encourages participants to examine their own cultural identities, leading to explorations of cultural assumptions, biases, and questions (Jurow, 2009). This is highly personal and vulnerable work, and the community in which such learning occurs can both support and impede the quality of knowledge constructed (Banks et al., 2007; Cochran-Smith, 2004). With this in mind, this book will focus on the construction of, enactment of, and lessons from RLCs that focus on the study of culture.

The field of multicultural education has long considered the theory and practice of teaching of culture. A most useful framework in this regard is James Banks's (2009) model of multicultural education that reflects four levels of integrating multicultural content into school curriculum: the contributions approach, the additive approach, the transformation approach, and the social action approach. In short, the contributions approach uses a rather superficial technique by focusing "on heroes, holidays, and cultural elements" (Banks, 2009, p. 238). Nothing is done to change the structure or goals of the course. In a sense, it is a nod to a surface level of culture. The additive approach goes one step deeper, adding "content, concepts, themes, and perspectives" without changing the curricular structure (p. 238). In this approach, a book or unit might be added without changing the course in any substantive way. The transformation approach "changes the basic assumptions of the curriculum and enables students to view concepts, issues, themes, and problems from several ethnic perspectives and points of view" (p. 242). In this approach, the nature of teaching and learning must shift to invite discussion, create the opportunity to voice multiple and differing perspectives, and encourage the understanding that a cultural artifact, belief, or value can be understood in many ways, depending on the life histories, cultural background, and ethnicities that are part of each person's life journey. The last approach is that of social action, which includes all the elements of the transformation approach but adds components that require students to make decisions and take actions related to the concept, issue, or problem studied in the unit (p. 245). Banks's model strongly informs the discussion that unfolds in this book.

The following chapters focus on the ways in which RLCs were cultivated in three summer seminars focusing on the teaching and learning of Jewish culture. The faculty team that developed and facilitated these seminars strived for the transformation approach through the particular relational-cultural pedagogies we chose (see Chapter 3), in addition to the particular ways that we defined the notion of text and the particular texts we selected to study (see Chapter 5). We hoped that the seminar would help the participants build the capacity and confidence to take action when they returned to their schools and home settings, thereby embracing the social action approach.

SUMMER SEMINARS: A RELATIONAL LEARNING COMMUNITY IN ACTION

To illustrate how an RLC can be constructed, enacted, and studied, I draw examples from these summer seminars and the model that we developed over 3 summers. In each seminar, intentional efforts were made to build an RLC with the participants and facilitators. The specific RLCs described within this volume serve as one model and can be used to imagine and implement RLCs in many different forms.

When planning our summer seminars, we selected one culture that could serve as an example for the study of other cultures. We chose to focus on Jewish culture, as it reflects an enduring and contemporary North American narrative (Lipset & Rabb, 1995; Sowell, 1983). The history of Jewish culture in the United States reflects key themes of multiculturalism in this country, including immigration, assimilation, marginalization, success, racism, and freedom (Whitfield, 1999, 2002). The endeavor of teaching about Jewish culture reflects a universal challenge of teaching about a specific culture—traversing common stereotypes and well-told stories to portray a more complex and nuanced narrative (Ball & Tyson, 2011).

It is important to claim my positionality in this choice as well. As the director of the Center for Studies in Jewish Education and Culture (CSJEC) at the University of Cincinnati, I have long been concerned with the ways that Jewish content and understandings are integrated into North American school curriculum. Often we see dimensions of Jewish history and culture taught in ancient civilization courses and not again until the teaching of the Holocaust. Surely there is much to be learned in the thousands of years between these two historical periods! In addition, common misconceptions about Jewish culture and religion persist, and bias and stereotypes are not uncommon in the lunchrooms, hallways, and sports fields of North American schools. Epithets such as "Is it true all Jews look for a deal?" "Don't Jew me down!" "You killed Jesus!" are still heard in school settings (e.g., Allen, 2016; Weiser, 2013). As an academic center in a public university, CSJEC's mission is to support the teaching and learning of Jewish history and culture in public, private, and parochial schools. In so doing, we seek to combat the anti-Semitism, racism, and ignorance that persist and to contribute to more just and peaceful schools. For me as a Jewish academic, and as a child of a Holocaust survivor and a German Jewish refugee, these goals are deeply personal as well as professional. Finally, it is important to recognize that these seminars were co-created with my husband and professional partner, Mark A. Raider, professor of modern Jewish history. As the cofounder of CSJEC, Mark contributed significantly to the historical orientation and pedagogy that were an essential cornerstone of this work. His passion for the teaching of Jewish history and culture was core to our cultural focus.

Curricular Goals

The relational/cultural orientation of the seminars was spelled out in our seminar syllabus:

> The philosophical orientation that guides the Summer Seminars emphasizes the relationship between the student, the teacher, other students, and texts that inspire genuine learning and excellent teaching. As such, the Seminar is rooted in an exploration of the place of Jewish text study in the learning and teaching process. Toward this end, the Seminar draws on a combination of traditional and modern Jewish texts . . . to examine the overlapping contexts within which institute participants live and work—that is, as teachers and educators in a variety of school settings that are a product of American society and, in some instances, Jewish life—and all of which have overt and/or indirect contact with Jews and the Jewish community. *We further posit that a close examination of American Jewish history and culture, the rich tapestry of Jewish texts, and the essential relationships of classroom life serve as a useful springboard for asking important questions about the place of Jews and other minorities in the lives of our students, schools, and society as a whole.* (2009, emphasis added)

As highlighted in the last sentence, the pedagogy, texts, and environment were guided by a relational orientation as well as cultural and historical ones. It is the combination of these orientations that characterize the curriculum and context of the seminars.

Participants

The participants in the seminars hailed from public middle and high schools, private secular and parochial schools (Jewish and Catholic), and supplementary and afternoon Jewish religious or Hebrew schools and represented a variety of teaching disciplines including social studies, language arts, mathematics, Judaic studies, the arts and music, foreign languages, Holocaust studies, and early childhood. The diversity of the group was also reflected in multiple religious backgrounds, countries of origin (e.g., United States, Israel, Argentina, Mexico, Nigeria), and race (Black, White, Latina, Asian). The participants' ages ranged from mid-20s to early 60s, and their teaching experience ranged from a few years to several decades. In addition, rabbinical students who had an interest in education and Jewish history joined the first two cohorts. The diversity of the group was essential to the construction of the seminars. Bringing multiple perspectives to the texts and discussions invited and facilitated a nuanced and complex inquiry. As we will see in Chapter 6, the participants identified this diversity as core to their learning.

In the chapters that follow, readers will "meet" many of the participants through narratives that were excerpted from their reflective work during the seminars, as well as from post-seminar interviews. Participants are all identified by pseudonym, but any mentions of the discipline they teach or setting in which they work are accurate. Additionally, they are identified by the year in which they enrolled in the seminars (2007, 2009, or 2010).

Texts

As discussed above, the relational triangle served as a central theoretical frame for the seminars, and the content or texts were essential "third partners" in the learning process. We chose to work with texts that are of ancient, modern, and contemporary origin and that reflect an expanded notion of text—including archival documents, film, photos, paintings, and physical spaces. A detailed discussion of our approach to texts will be discussed in Chapter 5, and Appendix C lists key sources we used. We selected texts that would invite multiple perspectives and divergent interpretations. In so doing, we reflected Banks's transformation approach, which sought to elicit diverse points of view, rooted in the life histories, stories, and frames of reference that individuals brought to the texts themselves.

Studying Our Practice

As research on teacher education is increasingly disconnected from teacher educators, this research answers Sleeter's (2014) urgent call that "teacher educators themselves be active shapers of a shared and usable research agenda on teacher education" (p. 146). Building on a series of practitioner inquiry studies conducted during and after each seminar, the model presented here is rooted in evidence of accounts by teachers of their own learning through reflective writing, in-depth interviews, and ethnographic observation. The goal of these studies was to inform both theory and practice in professional development. (For a full description of the theory and practice of the practitioner inquiry used throughout these studies, see Appendix B.) The research team for each seminar included some of the faculty/facilitators and doctoral students who joined yearlong research groups that conducted the follow-up interviews and analyzed the data. While I have written this book, the research upon which it is based was a collective effort. Readers will often see the pronoun *we* used to describe the work in the seminars—this reflects the strong team of faculty and graduate students who supported the teaching, learning, and research.

This book is based on cycles of practitioner inquiry that followed each of the seminars. Each cycle shaped the formation of the seminar that followed, and also contributed to the emerging knowledge regarding learning, relationship, and culture. Figure I.2 reflects the action research cycles and the scholarship that emerged. Detailed discussion of the methodology we implemented will be discussed in the Appendix B.

Implications for Action

What kind of changes were the seminars seeking to ignite? The summer seminars described in this volume sought to support teachers in strengthening their practice of teaching about cultural diversity in the United States. Recognizing that we inhabit an era of intense cultural conflict—whether we look to Syria, Ukraine/Russia, Sudan, Israel/Palestine, or closer to home, where racism and xenophobia are ever-present and appear to be on the rise—the seminars were created to help teachers construct both deeper content knowledge and pedagogies for the teaching of culture. By offering teachers the opportunity to study rich and challenging materials, in relationship and connection with their colleagues in the seminars, our model sought to provide teachers additional resources (understandings, pedagogies, materials) with which to return to their classrooms. Our hope was that they would be able to teach in ways that could address bias and misconceptions and help their students build deeper understandings and connections. In so doing, they would build and reinforce a notion of teacher as change agent.

Figure I.2. The Action Research Cycles of the Summer Seminars

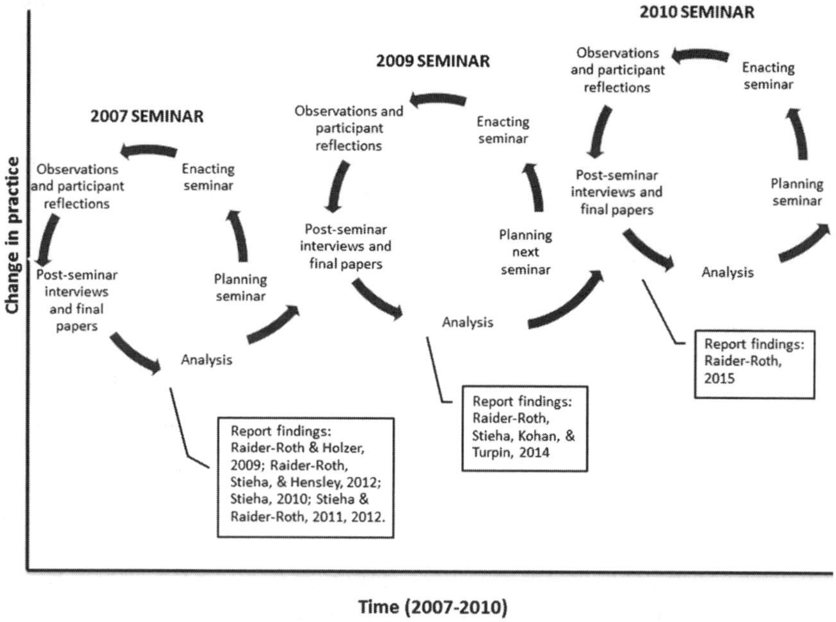

Source: Based on Raider-Roth, 2015; adapted from Muir, 2007

We convened 1-week summer seminars in order to create an intensive, intimate, and manageable learning experience. The curricular projects that some participants chose to implement following the seminar (those who had elected to enroll for graduate credit) reflected new curricular efforts based on the texts, practices, and pedagogies that were introduced. These projects provided a bridge of sorts to extend and deepen the learning from the RLC back into their classrooms, and a platform for pedagogical innovation. Since it was a 1-week seminar, we were conscious of the limitations of our capacity to actively support such action efforts. We also learned that the school context to which teachers returned had a large impact on their ability to act on what they learned in the seminar (Stieha, 2010; Stieha & Raider-Roth, 2011, 2012). For some, a supportive administration invited them to innovate—change their curricula, add new texts, experiment with new pedagogies. For others, they felt they had to put their learning and binders from the seminars "in a drawer." These accounts remind us of the centrality of context in teachers' capacity to innovate, grow, and learn.

STRUCTURE OF THE BOOK

The chapters in this volume will discuss the foundational dimensions of RLCs that focus on the teaching and learning of culture. These dimensions are interconnected and dependent upon one another to build the vibrancy and energy of an RLC. Yet in order to describe each of these dimensions, I have separated them out in the chapters to come. Thus, readers will notice frequent cross references between chapters. For example, when relational-cultural pedagogies are discussed (Chapter 3), I refer to the dimension of texts (Chapter 5) and the practices of supporting, challenging, and voicing (Chapter 4). Such cross-references aim to remind readers of the wholeness of the RLC model and assist them in making important connections as they read.

The volume begins with a discussion of the relational demands of culturally oriented professional development in Chapter 1. In creating a relationally healthy and trusting environment, teachers were able to ask hard questions of themselves and one another. The theoretical underpinnings that guided our construction of these practices will be delineated. In addition, the practice or enactment of these principles in the seminars will be described.

Chapter 2 unpacks the notion of relational awareness as a core capacity for teacher educators. I argue that the capacity to detect participants' dynamics of connection and disconnection within RLCs is crucial to support transformative learning. These dynamics can occur with self, peers, facilitators, texts, and context. This kind of attunement is essential in facilitating repair or reconnection when inevitable ruptures occur.

In Chapter 3, I describe the relational-cultural pedagogies of hevruta text study, descriptive process, and historiographic inquiry that can support communal study of culturally oriented texts. This chapter will also discuss the seminar participants' responses to these practices and the ways in which they supported and thwarted participants' learning. These practices share five theoretical and pedagogical facets, including holding the relational triangle at their core, supporting participants' capacity to be present, inviting close looking at focal texts, slowing down the interpretive process, and offering the possibility of transformative learning.

Chapter 4 will describe the set of practices of supporting, challenging, and voicing, and how they serve core relational needs for the adult learning process. It will explore how supporting and challenging—what Robert Kegan (1994) describes as essential in human development—are the interpersonal ethical responsibilities that learners share with one another. It will also examine how voicing (Gilligan, 2011; Linklater, 1976) begins in this interpersonal space and migrates to the intrapersonal space, where acts of authoring and agency can be enacted.

As described above, the choice of texts is significant. Chapter 5 will discuss in greater depth the rationale for and the kinds of materials (i.e., texts) that offer easily accessible opportunities for becoming third partners in the learning process. In particular, I offer an expanded notion of "text" to include film, art, and place.

Research based on the summer seminars suggests that participants found themselves examining aspects of their personal, professional, and cultural identities. Chapter 6 illustrates the kinds of identity challenges and shifts that can occur in culturally focused RLCs. Rooted in transformative learning theory (Mezirow, 2012; Kegan, 1994), this chapter will discuss why such identity examinations are necessary and unavoidable parts of transformative learning.

The book closes with a discussion and recommendations for practice concerning culturally specific forms of professional development. Guidelines for constructing courses, workshops, and summer institutes are found in Appendix A. Appendix B offers a relational-cultural practitioner inquiry framework for teacher educators who wish to study their own practice. A sampling of texts used throughout the seminars is available in Appendix C.

It is my hope that this volume can inform the work of teacher educators and professional development facilitators who seek to deepen their understandings of the relational dynamics and demands that can occur in professional development settings. In addition, this book can be useful and supportive for all who teach in higher education classrooms and wish to build strong relational contexts in which transformative learning can emerge.

The findings described in these chapters—detailed through narratives, stories, and analyses—make the case for creating teachers' professional learning environments that are deep, extended, collective, and relational spaces in which serious study of culture takes place. Such intellectual and relational engagement can help support teachers in locating and enacting their visions of democratic education.

Relationships in Context

Foundations for Teacher Learning

The idea of a relational learning community (RLC) is grounded in both theory and practice. The focus of this chapter is to consider how attention to and care for the environment/context/setting is a foundational step in creating RLCs. In addition, the discussion focuses on how RLCs can be seen as a form of democratic praxis that can support teachers' capacities to imagine and enact change in their classrooms and schools. Finally, I will describe core components for building the environment of the RLC.

The concepts of learning spaces, environment, and context are core to successful growth-enhancing experiences. Relational theorists have long considered environment as central to growth and development. D. W. Winnicott (1960) coined the term "holding environment" to describe the space in which infants grow within relationships with their parents. He argues that without "good enough" holding, development "cannot be attained" or "established" (p. 589). Robert Kegan (1994) builds on this idea in considering adult development and explains the holding environment as providing

> both welcoming acknowledgment to exactly who the person is right now as he or she is, and fosters the person's psychological evolution. As such, a holding environment is a tricky transitional culture, an evolutionary bridge, a context for crossing over. (p. 43)

Conceptualizing the holding environment as an evolutionary bridge, Kegan helps us understand the necessity of a context that can support growth, that can support a "crossing over" to new ways of thinking and new knowledge. Such environments are crucial in adult learning because developing new ways of thinking necessitates a destabilization of what a person knows. Destabilization is widely recognized as an unavoidable (and often unpleasant) part of transformative learning processes. Kegan (1994) labels this a state of "disequilibrium," while Dewey refers to it as a "felt difficulty" (1910/1933) and Mezirow (2012) defines it as a "disorienting dilemma." Moments such as these (extended or momentary) are pivotal points in which a person can choose to flee the learning setting, shut down so as to quiet the internal dissonance that can be experienced, or "face" the situation in a cycle of reflective thought (Dewey, 1910/1933).

Dewey (1963) theorized the centrality of environment in the learning process as well:

> A primary responsibility of educators is that they not only be aware of the general principle of the shaping of actual experience by environing conditions, but that they also recognize in the concrete what surroundings are conducive to having experiences that lead to growth. Above all, they should know how to utilize the surroundings, physical and social, that exist so as to extract from them all that they have to contribute to building up experiences that are worthwhile. (p. 40)

Dewey's conception highlights the importance of teachers' awareness of how the environment mediates students' learning as well as their responsibility for constructing an environment that can help generate valuable learning experiences. It is worth underscoring that Dewey defines the environment as including the *surroundings*, the *physical* and the *social*. "The environment," he explains, "is whatever conditions interact with personal needs, desires, purposes, and capacities to create the experience which is had" (p. 44). The environment, then, is malleable as it interacts with the learners and is shaped by their engagement with it.

Building on Dewey's, Kegan's, and Winnicott's ideas of environment and holding environment, the context within which the professional development occurs is essential to an RLC. This context shapes and is shaped by the learners within. Teacher educators in an RLC pay attention to the physical space and its conduciveness to learning. Can people move around easily? Can they see each other? Can the space accommodate different groupings—whole-group, small-group, pairs? Do the acoustics allow for small-group talking so that all members can hear one another? RLC educators pay attention to the physical needs of the learners. Are the chairs comfortable? Is the schedule such that people can move their bodies? Does the space accommodate differently abled learners? Finally, RLC educators pay attention to the social context. What does it take for strangers to get to know each other? What experiences facilitate or impede the building of social connection? All these facets of environment can both invite connections and trigger disconnections (with self, others, and content) for participants. As will be explored in Chapter 2, becoming attuned to these dynamics of connection and disconnection is key to developing relational awareness. Paying close attention to the ways that *context* or holding environment can facilitate and disrupt relational connections is part of such awareness. Each of the dimensions of context described in this chapter is an opportunity to attend to the dynamics of connection.

RELATIONSHIPS, COMMUNITY, AND DEMOCRACY

The holding environment of the RLC shapes and is shaped by the quality of relationships of the members of the community. Let us begin by addressing the question "Why relationships?" Learning relationships are the cornerstone of the formation of new knowledge. Prior research has demonstrated that in order to construct trustworthy knowledge, learners must be engaged in trustworthy relationships (Raider-Roth, 2005a). What do we mean by learning relationships? Jean Baker Miller (1986) defines characteristics of growth-enhancing relationships as including "five good things." Each person in the relationship "feels a greater sense of 'zest,'" "feels more able to act and does act," " has a more accurate picture of her/himself and the other person(s)," "feels a greater sense of worth," and "feels more connected to the other person(s) and feels energized to pursue other relationships" (p. 3). In addition to the feelings that connote a growth-enhancing relationship, Miller and Stiver (1997) argue that the signpost of development is the capacity to develop and grow "into" relationships (rather than the dominant Western cultural view of maturity as symbolized by separation). Building on this view of growth and development, I understand the "relational" component of the RLC to be nurturing these "five good things" and supporting individual teachers to deepen their capacity to learn in relationship with their colleagues.

In the past 10 years, I have also come to see healthy learning relationships as central to our capacity to live democratically. Such relationships are ones in which new ideas, innovative thinking, and creative expression can thrive. My understandings begin in the work of John Dewey. In *Democracy and Education*, he wrote:

> A democracy is primarily a mode of associated living, of conjoint communicated experience. The extension in space of the number of individuals who participate in an interest so that each has to refer to his own action to that of others, and to consider the action of others to give point and direction to his own, is equivalent to the breaking down of those barriers of class, race and national territory which kept men from perceiving the full import of activity. (1916/1966, p. 87)

Here Dewey teaches us that democracy is a way of living with others, a way of being in relationship, where each person's actions shape and are shaped by the actions of others. Such connection breaks down the barriers that divide us, that hold us back, that keep us out of growth-enhancing relationships.

Dewey helps us understand that one must learn to live in a democracy—this is the essential work of schools. A primary job of teachers is to help students construct experiences in which democratic dispositions and habits can be practiced. How do teachers learn to create such environments, especially if they have not experienced democratic learning communities in their own schooling or in their teaching lives? The adage "You can't teach what you don't know" rings true here. As teacher educators, we must attend to the current reality in which many teachers reside—schools in which democratic principles are absent, fading, or holding on for dear life, as the mandates for standardization drown out the possibility for change, adaptation, and responsiveness. Hence, it is even more urgent that learning settings for teachers embrace Dewey's principles of democracy, so that the embodied, lived experience of learning can be brought back to their own classroom lives.

It is in the formation of community that democracy can be practiced and learned. Cuffaro (1995) helps us understand Dewey's meaning:

> It is when these different memberships [in diverse groups], with their varied perspectives, can be interwoven into a fabric of shared meanings and aspirations that community is born—when each person making his or her unique contribution participates in an undertaking meaningful to each and inclusive of all. For Dewey, the community that supports such movement and existence is a democracy. (p. 26)

Not only does community need to be a tapestry for meaning-making and participation in which the individual is invited to the construction of a greater whole, it also thrives when the voices of the members' diversity can be shared. Cuffaro further explains:

> [Dewey's] vision of democracy welcomes plurality and diversity and rejects barriers that divide and exclude. Accepting the spirit of Dewey's vision, we are challenged to attend to whatever diminishes the growth of a democratic society and to whatever silences voices, voices needed for participants and communication are vital to a growing community. (p. 103)

Dewey's charge—to attend to whatever diminishes the growth of a democratic society—is one echoed today by relational psychologists. Carol Gilligan argues in her recent scholarship (2003, 2011, 2014, 2016) that democracy "rests on a presumption of equal voice or equality" (2014, p. 95). In Gilligan's work, we hear the steady and clear message that, like love, "democracy depend[s] on voice" (2003, p. 229), returning us to Dewey, for whom "communication" is essential to democracy. Like Dewey, Gilligan argues that the biggest threat to democracy is the silencing of voice, and the forces that split us, rendering some with voice and some without. Thus, the formation of community, where each member can voice her ideas, emerging questions, and disagreements, is where the work of democracy can begin, and where learning that can change the fabric of our culture can begin as well.

The relationships that form the fabric of these learning communities must be rooted in empathy, which is "the ability to identify with the feelings and perspectives of others . . . and to respond appropriately" (Gordon, 2009, p. 30). Adding the reciprocal dimension of empathy, relational-cultural theorists describe mutual empathy similarly, as the capacity to be with another person in thinking, feeling, and action (Miller & Stiver, 1997). Mary Gordon, creator of the high-impact program Roots of Empathy, (2009), explains that empathy is both a cognitive and an affective skill that must be taught. Learning to take the perspectives of others is part and parcel of this work. As such, we can hear the echoes of democratic practice in the work of empathy.

ENACTING COMMUNITY AND DIVERSITY

As discussed above, Dewey teaches us that diversity in community is an important step in living democratically. Cuffaro (1995) helps us understand Dewey's teaching more specifically. She explains: "It is when these different memberships, with their varied perspectives, can be interwoven into a fabric of shared meanings and aspirations that community is born" (p. 26). In this Deweyan view, true community requires pluralistic views, people from multiple walks of life. Cuffaro continues:

> Potential and capacity require an environment that invites realization, and individuality is fostered in a community that celebrates plurality as a means for renewal. Diversity extends the scope of community, enlarges and elaborates its meanings (p. 27).

Dewey teaches us that in learning environments whose goal is that of democracy, building community is a foundational step to bridging divides, unbuilding walls of division, and making space for polyvocal expression. Garrison (1996) underscores this Deweyan notion of diversity and community:

> It is not until a person meets with the differences of another's point of view that she can recognize her own habits and prejudices, much less inquire about them. We can know ourselves only if we know others different from ourselves, and others different from ourselves only if we know ourselves. That is why pluralistic democracy is the best form of community. (p. 449)

In learning with those who are different from one's self, the potential for growth is heightened—including knowledge of self and knowledge of the other. In this way, we see that democratic practice has the potential for transformative learning.

Indeed, Mezirow (2012), one of the principal theorists of transformative learning theory, argues that "there is a reciprocity between democratic theory and transformation theory" (p. 91). He explains that educators of adult learners "create protected learning environments in which the conditions of social democracy necessary for transformative learning are fostered" (p. 93).[1] A protected environment is not one without disagreement, or disruption. In fact, it is an environment that invites the critical reflection on and unsettling of personal frames of reference and habits of mind. This is where democracy and transformation come together. Through this discussion, we can see how RLCs can be holding environments for democratic praxis.

ENACTMENT: SUMMER SEMINAR RLC PRACTICES AND PROCESSES

In this section I offer concrete practices for building the environment in our seminars, which are based in the theories described in the first part of the chapter. My effort is not to suggest that these are the only practices that can accomplish these goals but, rather, that these were useful in the construction of our RLCs. As in all the chapters that follow, participants' reflections are woven throughout the text so that their understandings of their learning and experience is an integral part of the narrative.

In constructing the RLC in our summer seminars, we viewed it as a holding environment for the participants and faculty, as an "evolutionary bridge" for each person and for the group (Kegan, 1994). This meant an environment in which hard questions could be asked, risks taken, and new ideas constructed. Lynn [2010],[2] a curriculum coordinator in a charter school, reflected what we were hoping to create:

> I felt like I was able to take risks and get a little deeper because of the safeness of the environment and the means in which we looked at the various texts we were presented with.

Sonia [2009], a director of an afternoon religious school, described the kind of relational group-building that occurred in order to do the challenging work that was asked of the participants:

> Well, I think we did a lot of development work to lower our barriers, to trust each other, and to be able to challenge and be challenged. You know, if you go to that place, it opens up the soft side of you.

By emphasizing the notion of "safeness," "trust," and "lowering barriers," Lynn and Sonia highlight requisite relational dynamics for learning. Other participants identified these dynamics as well, using terms such as "safety net," "open environment conducive to trust," and "safe space."

Referring to challenging practices (see Chapter 4), Sonia highlights that the actual work of learning was not always about being in harmony, but was about expanding "horizons" and ways of seeing. The concept of safety did not mean that everyone agreed, but rather that it was "safe enough to be dangerous" (Butterwick, 2002, p. 248).[3] For some participants this meant letting go of the notion of "consensus," or in the words of Marie [2009], the "false promise of group harmony." It was the airing of differences, multiple perspectives, and varied ways of understanding one text that invited the safety to learn.

Physical Space

Each seminar was held at the Jacob Rader Marcus Center of the American Jewish Archives on the Hebrew Union College–Jewish Institute of Religion Cincinnati campus (AJA).[4] We chose this space because of the unparalleled access the AJA offered in terms of primary texts that could be studied by each seminar. In addition, and centrally important, there was the conference room in which we studied. A sunlit space, with doors to an outside patio, this room offered a sense of professionalism and comfort. Parallelogram-shaped wooden tables offered flexibility for large-group as well as small-group and paired learning.

Confidence-Building Experiences

We began each seminar with icebreakers, the tried-and-true approach to building learning groups. From all our experiences as teachers, camp counselors, and teacher educators, the faculty knew this was a useful way to begin—it was important for all members of the group to get to know one another. There was nothing novel about this idea. We began with the usual introductions—what brought you here, what is one thing you hope to learn, what are your expectations, what is one thing that no one in the group knows about you? We also built in more playful experiences—such as "speed dating" with getting-to-know-you prompts, and wine/fruit juice tastings. Interestingly, the participants noted these experiences as important to their learning in the seminars. Marie [2009], a language arts teacher at a Catholic middle school, described the icebreakers as "confidence-building activities" that "were very helpful because it made me feel like I was able to be a part of the group and not isolated from the group." We found this comment striking, as it reinforced the idea that building connection with the group would also help individuals build confidence or trust in themselves. Cathy [2010], a veteran English teacher in an urban high school, reflected, "All the icebreakers, mixing it up, musical chairs, you-call-on-the-next-person-using-our names help remind us that learning is *personal*, and the more open and trusting we are, the more we will learn" [emphasis in the original].

Both Marie's and Cathy's comments highlight the relationship between the individual learner and the community, the personal and the professional. They reinforce a central Deweyan idea: Openness is a prerequisite for learning and growth (Garrison, 1996). Fundamental experiences such as learning one another's names and getting to know something about people's home lives, talents, and worries all contribute to the capacity for openness.

Community Singing

One practice that our faculty member Elie Holzer brought to the seminar was that of singing. Each seminar, we selected one song to begin or end our day. In the 1st year, the song was in Hebrew (with transliterated pronunciations and translation provided); in subsequent years, we chose a *niggun*—a Jewish wordless melody, meant to draw participants into the spirit of learning. Our original intention in bringing song to the seminar was to help build group cohesiveness as well as provide an immersive experience of Jewish culture. Our research indicated that the participants found this practice both unnerving and important. In her end-of-seminar reflection, Karen [2010], a middle school English teacher, wrote of the singing:

> While this certainly put me out of my comfort zone at times, I feel as though it helped the group to bond together. Having a shared time together to focus our thoughts was important. We were forced to be present.

Karen's comment highlights both the discomfort that this practice surfaced and the bringing together of individuals to the communal. Interestingly, she comments that the practice "forced" her to be present. While she does not comment on the object of her presence (self, others, texts), the shared time to focus was part of the presence stance. Sue [2009], a teacher in a Catholic high school, commented, "The *niggun* felt awkward at first even though I know other tunes. As the week went on, the singing became a nonverbal expression of our delight in studying together." As for Karen and many participants across the seminars, the singing was often "uncomfortable," "awkward," "out of comfort zones," and "forced," yet it led to a sense of pleasure and community, tying together process, content, and learning. Megan [2009], a preschool teacher in a Jewish community center, commented on this sense of connection: "I thought that the use of the *niggun* helped us connect to one another and the pieces we were learning." For Corinne [2009], a teacher at a public middle school, the singing

> built a sense of community by drawing us together in a universal language (music). The music Elie chose was what I identified from my background knowledge as Jewish in sound. But with no actual words

> being used, everyone was invited to join. I found it to be the auditorial identification of the community we had formed as this particular group of learners.

Brad [2010], a social studies teacher, concurred: "I feel that the singing was a community builder, which in turn caused [us] to feel more comfortable sharing our ideas with each other during other activities." Brad's and Corinne's comments highlight the capacity for singing and music to contribute to the construction of a learning community.

Shared Meals

My graduate students often tease me that they know whenever I teach, there will be food. As is commonly known, in many communities, the sharing of food is part of community-building. This is also true in the culture of teaching. Symbolically, teachers need nourishment. Working in a caregiving job, they themselves need to be cared for, in order to keep up their energy and zest for the hard work that they do. While the sharing of food can raise complexities (such food allergies and sensitivities) and it is vitally important to be attentive to these issues, collective meals invite the possibility for forming relationships that can support learning. While food is often a large item in our budget sheets, it is clearly a necessary "material" for learning. Martina [2010], an administrator at a Jewish educational agency, reflected on this idea in her end-of-seminar reflection: "I really appreciated the care taken to ensure the 'creature comforts'—this truly helped to support the learning by creating an atmosphere conducive for it." Brad [2010] detailed how these shared meals helped create such an atmosphere:

> Oddly, I feel that the meals which we shared together were especially useful/productive/inspiring. Our conversations with regards to Jewish culture and pedagogy often spilled over into mealtime. Also, like the singing, these meals allowed us to form a "safe community . . . in which it is safe enough to say something that is dangerous."

The space that mealtimes provided to continue discussions from the sessions, and to take risks in a more informal setting, contributed to the construction of the learning community. Brad's last comments also underscore the place that the discussion of group norms played into building the learning community.

Shared Norms for Learning

Articulating shared norms for learning is a core practice in any learning environment that I facilitate. The purpose of this practice is the articulation of hidden assumptions (for an example of a norm-setting protocol, see McDonald, Mohr, Dichter, & McDonald, 2014). The cultural assumptions around norms for discussions are diverse. As I often relate in discussions concerning norms, it was commonplace in my childhood home for us to interrupt one another as we talked during mealtimes. This was part of the rhythm of the meal. Yet I had friends who spoke only when they were asked to by a parent. During norm-setting sessions at the seminar, I asked participants to articulate the kinds of dynamics that support their learning. In addition to engendering frequent responses such as "listening," "respect," and "interrupting," I was certain to raise the question of how to handle disagreement. If a core goal was supporting each participant's articulation of voice, then it was important to talk about how to disagree. As Debold, Tolman, and Brown (1996) wrote, "the given ground of disagreement" is an important bedrock for learning. While for some participants the act of public disagreement was natural, for others it was highly uncomfortable.

Daily Reflection and Sikkum

RLCs create regular opportunities for reflection on both the process of learning and the focal content. It is important for participants to be able to "keep their fingers on their pulse" and have moments to check in personally and comment on their learning process. It is also important for the group as a whole to reflect collectively on how the group is functioning and ways in which the group can better support the members' learning.

During the summer seminars, we used three different forms of reflection during the week for different purposes. The first, *individual reflection*, often done in the form of journal writing, offered the individual learners opportunities to track their learning, associations, questions, discomforts, new ideas, and other issues. The second, *collaborative reflection*, was meant to help the participants inform one another and the facilitators about their learning processes, the challenges they confronted, and the questions they encountered. These written reflections—often shared daily—would help the facilitators adjust the pedagogy and experiences to address participants' evolving needs and concerns. In this way, the pedagogy was responsive and evolving. The third form of reflection, *collective reflection*, was publicly shared, in order to help the community convey ways in which the learning processes were proceeding. These were often shared immediately following an exercise, practice, or experience. Another version of collective reflection was one that I shared daily and at the end of the week. I called this the *sikkum* (Hebrew for "summary") and was a practice I learned from Vito Perrone (1933–2011), esteemed professor of education at the Harvard Graduate School of Education and founder of the North Dakota Study Group on Evaluation (NDSG).[5] At the end of NDSG conferences, Vito sat in front of the group and offered a perspective on what had happened during the previous 3 days. With an uncanny capacity for observation, he would recall important conversations, controversies, questions, humorous moments, and thematic threads that had run throughout the conference. Though no one can replicate Vito's wisdom, I emulated his capacity to "hold the whole" for the group, to reflect back, much like a mirror, what had occurred during the day. Each day was so jam-packed, sometimes it was hard for people to see the connections between everything that had occurred. Asking the participants to sit back and relax, I read the sikkum aloud. Sometimes participants contributed to the sikkum, or volunteered to present a sikkum in another form, such as a word cloud or wordle.[6] The purpose was the same—to synthesize themes, questions, and big ideas that occurred. (For an example of a sikkum, see Chapter 2.)

Each form of reflection was important in the construction of the RLC. The individual form invited participants to pause, to "touch base" with themselves, to make sure that their needs were being met. The collaborative form offered participants the opportunity to share their concerns with the facilitators and with one another, thereby helping to co-create a responsive curriculum. The collective form both encouraged and reminded participants that an RLC required the voices of all participants in order to be a democratic space.

Group Composition

Diversity of the learning group was a core feature of each seminar. While in 2010 we achieved the most diverse group (from a demographic perspective), each seminar was intentionally planned to bring together teachers from different settings, backgrounds, and life experiences. In 2007, half the group were Jewish day school teachers (though not all were Jewish) and the other half were rabbinical students. In this way, some participants brought Jewish text–subject matter expertise while others brought pedagogical–subject matter expertise. Our second seminar in 2009 brought teachers from public, private, parochial, and secular schools from across Ohio (and two teachers from Florida). By 2010, through the generosity of the Posen Foundation, we were able to open our doors nationally. Teachers traveled from across the United States, hailing from public, private, parochial, and secular schools. While I will discuss in Chapter 6 the ways in which the diversity of the group itself contributed to a sense of transformative learning, I raise the diversity of the group composition as core to the ways we built a learning community.

SUMMARY

This chapter reflects both the theories and practices that contributed to the ways the seminars built an RLC each summer. The notion of a "holding environment" for learning was central to building a space in which the participants' assumptions could be challenged, where voices could be articulated, and where new ideas could be supported. Practices, including confidence-building experiences, songs, shared meals, and group norms, were central to the construction of this community. Similarly, building a group with diverse cultural backgrounds, life experiences, religious affiliations, subject matter expertise, and pedagogical orientations supported a group in which multiple perspectives were invited, needed, and amplified in order to build deep understandings. Such diversity is core to a democratic praxis, where learning in relationship can support our capacity to take action for a more just society.

CHAPTER 2

Relational Awareness

Learning to See Connection and Disconnection and Facilitate Reconnection

The work of professional development facilitators/teacher educators is complex and requires a diverse and deep tool set. In addition to constructing a learning environment that is conducive to building a relational learning community (RLC), we must develop the core capacity of relational awareness. Judith Jordan (2004) defines relational awareness as

> the development of clarity about the movement of relationship; this importantly includes an awareness of our patterns and ways of connecting and disconnecting, and transforming the flow from the direction of disconnection to connection. It includes personal awareness, awareness of the other, awareness of the impact of oneself on the other, the effect of other on oneself, and the quality of energy and flow in the relationship itself. (pp. 53–54)

Jordan's definition highlights that the flow of relationship is one that includes moments of connection, disconnection, and reconnection. To become relationally aware is to become attuned to one's own connections and disconnections with self as well as with others. In RLCs, I argue that we also need to become attuned to the relationships with our subject matter (or texts) as well as the community/context at large. In a sense, relational awareness is becoming attuned to each of the segments in the relational triangle, as well as the ways in which the context/culture shapes and is shaped by the triangle itself.

The need for relational awareness is well argued in the fields of psychotherapy (Jordan, 2010), counseling (Comstock et al., 2008), counselor education (Duffey, 2006), and group process (Jordan & Dooley, 2000). Yet its application in the world of teacher education generally and professional development more specifically has yet to be fully explored. In this chapter, I argue that relational awareness is a core capacity for leaders/facilitators of RLCs. I will explore how becoming attuned to connection, disconnection, and repair (or reconnection) are foundational aspects of relational awareness.

Understanding what it takes to become relationally aware or attuned has been examined over the past few decades, largely in the work of Judith

Jordan, Jean Baker Miller, Irene Stiver, and others (e.g., Miller & Stiver, 1997; Jordan, 2004, 2010). More recently, complementary terms that tilt toward this notion of capacity for relational understanding have also been identified—terms such as *relational competence*, *relational confidence*, *relational-cultural mindfulness*, and *relational empowerment* (Jordan, 1992, 2010; Jordan & Dooley, 2000; Surrey & Kramer, 2013). I have chosen the concept of *relational awareness* as particularly important in the work of RLCs, because being alert to the "energy" and "flow" of the relationships in RLCs is foundational to building a holding environment in which transformational learning can take place. Being able to detect when connections are thriving and healthy, when they might be more fragile and frayed, and finding strategies for reconnection are key capacities to support the health and functioning of an RLC.

Relational awareness as a facilitator of an RLC is akin to being "present with" and looking at one's patterns of relating; one has a modicum of distance and capacity to observe at the same time one is present in the experience. There is an attunement to self, other, and relational processes. Awareness involves a nonjudgmental stance, an ability to notice and observe without becoming totally immersed or caught in the experience. One can learn to see consequences and sequences of behaviors without moving into paralyzing self-doubt and self-blame (Jordan 2004, p. 54).

By highlighting the synergy between relational awareness and presence, Jordan offers a bridge between relational-cultural theory—which is rooted in psychology and the therapeutic process—and the work of RLC facilitators. While we will discuss this in greater depth in Chapter 3, it is important to introduce the notion of presence here (Chu, 2014; Rodgers & Raider-Roth, 2006; Stieha & Raider-Roth, 2012). Presence to self, other, text, and context is critical to relational-cultural pedagogies. When enacting or leading these pedagogies, RLC facilitators strive to assume a stance of relational awareness, or presence with the participants. While we create opportunities for participants to practice observation and a nonjudgmental stance toward self, others, and the text (via relational-cultural pedagogies), we too must practice a similar stance. By looking for evidence of connection, disconnection, and repair, we can be alert to and take appropriate action to support connection, minimize disconnections, and facilitate repair. In the rest of this chapter, we will both examine theoretical understandings of connection, disconnection, and repair, and illustrate what these relational states can look like in action.

DEFINING CONNECTION

To connect in relationships means to reach outside ourselves to tune in, to be present, to see the "other," and to respond empathically. Jean Baker

Miller and Irene Stiver (1997) define connection as "an interaction between two or more people that is mutually empathic and mutually empowering" (p. 26). They suggest that when a person is "in" connection with another there is an increase "in a feeling of vitality, aliveness, energy"—an emotion they label as "zest" (p. 30). Zest is one element of "five good things" that occur when two people experience a relationship based on mutual empowerment. The other "good things" include having the ability to act, a more accurate image of self, a greater sense of self-worth, and more energy to stay in and seek out relationships (Miller, 1986, p. 3.).

When I teach about connection and disconnection in my graduate seminars, the issue of mutuality is often contested. How can a relationship between a teacher and a student be mutual? The power differentials as well as the difference in roles and responsibilities seem to contradict a common understanding of mutuality—a sense of equal give-and-take. In a teaching-learning relationship, mutuality looks different. In a connected teaching-learning relationship teachers facilitate the learning opportunities, set up the environment, and provide important feedback to their students. They are also observing, tracking, and looking for evidence that students are engaging in these experiences and constructing new knowledge. The forms of feedback that teachers receive from students—oral and written reflection on students' learning processes, dialogue with teachers about their work and learning, and so forth—constitute a form of "giving back" to the teacher. Amy Banks (2006) argues that mutuality in a client-therapist relationship involves the client being "able to see that she has an impact on the therapist; the client can see the therapist moved by her subjective experience" (p. 28). Extrapolating this idea to the teacher-student relationship, I suggest that mutuality occurs when students can see that they have had an impact on the teacher—that the teacher has learned from the student. This fluidity of role of teacher and learner—or the I and Thou (in Hawkins's words)—pushes back against the traditional notion of teacher as expert or all-knowing, and promotes a more equitable conception of the teacher-learner relationship.

We also understand the idea of deepening connection with one's self as a relational concept, where this self-understanding and development is necessarily embedded in relationships. A crucial link between relationships and connection with self is the notion of authenticity. Miller and Stiver (1997) define authenticity as "a person's ongoing ability to represent her-/himself in a relationship with increasing truth and fullness" (p. 54). Teachers in RLCs can thus nurture connection to self by creating and participating in environments that support their authenticity—their ability to bring their full selves to the table.

When thinking about a person's connection to text, it is helpful to turn to Elie Holzer, who guides us through the philosophies of Hans Gadamer and Paul Ricoeur. Holzer (2016) argues that "the interpretive encounter with texts can move the reader in two directions: a backward direction in making her aware of some of her prejudices and a forward direction, in causing her to deepen, expand or alter her own view of the topic" (p. 29). This understanding of connectedness to text calls forth both the emotional and intellectual dimensions of this kind of engagement. It is an engagement that asks learners/readers to locate themselves in the past, present, and future.

Finally, what is meant by connection to the environment or context? It is a recognition that the culture around us (both locally and more globally) shapes and is shaped by the relationships within. Connection to the environment or context means understanding that "connections form or fail to form within a web of other social and cultural relationships" (Jordan & Walker, 2004, p. 4). The forces of culture—both positive and negative—can both support and impede individuals' capacities to build relationships with one another, and such awareness is crucial if we are to try to transform the cultural pressures that inhibit growth. Such cultural pressures include hierarchical "power over" relationships, where power is used to direct and control, signified by the pernicious "isms" of our culture, the Western culture that often elevates separation over connection. These are forces of disconnection, forces that interrupt growth and resilience.

DEFINING DISCONNECTION

The notion of disconnection in teachers' learning is a relatively unexplored area of research. What causes teachers to retreat or otherwise disconnect from themselves, from their learning partners, teacher educators, and the focal texts of study? Understanding the sources of disconnections, developing the awareness to detect breaks in relationship, and building strategies for reconnection (termed as "repair" in the relational literature) are crucial capacities for teacher educators in supporting teachers' learning.

Let's begin with a clear understanding of disconnection. Miller and Stiver (1997) define such breaks as occurring "whenever a relationship is not mutually empathic and mutually empowering (which means we experience disconnections often.) The degree of disconnection can vary from a very minor feeling of being out of touch to major trauma and violation." Disconnection means "a break in connection accompanied by a sense of being cut off from the other person[s]" (p. 51). A sense of depletion accompanies disconnection and can be viewed as "simply the opposite of the five good things" (Comstock et al., 2008, p. 282). Disconnection, therefore, is experienced as a decrease in energy, a sense of being stuck or unable to act, confusion or cloudy thinking, a reduced sense of self-worth, and waning desire to remain in relationships. Disconnections can be minor, momentary ruptures when a learning partner misunderstands or tunes out. While less severe in nature, these episodes can momentarily derail the learning process.

If they occur consistently, then they become more acute, and learning can be impeded (Raider-Roth, 2005a).

Building on Miller and Stiver's conception of disconnection, Jordan (2010) broadens the definition by addressing cultural forces of disconnection: "Racism, homophobia, class prejudice and sexism all lead to chronic disconnections that create pain and drain energy in individuals and societies" (pp. 5–6). Disconnections of this kind can have severe consequences. In addition to the pain and energy drain to which Jordan refers, they can impede people's capacity to learn, to construct knowledge, and to exercise agency in a learning setting. Because of this, learners do not experience success in these domains, and their capacity to participate in society and democracy can be compromised. Comstock and colleagues (2008) echo Jordan's argument in the context of counseling:

> The context of relational development across the life span is inextricably linked to individuals' racial/cultural/social identities. As such, examining culture-based relational disconnections is one way to promote counselors' relational, multicultural and social justice counseling competencies. (p. 280)

Comstock and colleagues' work in counseling practice can inform teacher educators' work by helping us learn to locate both relational and cultural disconnections, and supporting our educational social justice competencies. When we become alert to and understand the ways that forces of culture can cause disconnected moments in learning, we can take action, working to mend the rifts through a just and democratic stance.

Disconnections often reflect a relational paradox. On the one hand, they can compromise a person's learning and growth. On the other, an individual might choose to, or reflexively, disconnect as a form of resistance to a system or a moment that is experienced as oppressive or threatening. Much as a sea anemone will fold in its flowerlike tentacles when it is touched or a threat is perceived, humans can retreat when the environment feels unsafe. Thus a disconnection can be a self-protective move. Therein lies the paradox—a disconnection can protect an individual and at the same time compromise the person's capacity to grow and learn (Gilligan, 1996, 2011; Miller & Stiver, 1997).

REPAIR

> No matter how specialized we are, how technically oriented, we are bound to think about remaking and repairing. We wonder—and how can we help it?—how best to renew. (Greene, 1982)

An important counterpart of disconnection is *repair* or *reparation*. Originally conceptualized in the literature on infancy, repair was viewed as a necessary form of communication between the infant and the caregiver, occurring after a disconnection transpires, such as when an infant cries in response to hunger and the caregiver does not immediately detect the need (Tronick, 1989, 2007). As the caregiver responds to different cues from the infant and figures out the infant's needs, the infant modifies her communication so as to elicit the caregiver's responses more quickly. In this interaction, both caregiver and infant develop stronger communication capacities and are empowered by their newly found abilities to be in sync with one another. This cycle of communication, called the Mutual Regulation Model (Tronick, 2007; Tronick & Weinberg, 1997), has strong implications for the teacher-student relationship (Murray, 2005; Raider-Roth, 2005a) and the teacher educator-participant relationship (Raider-Roth et al., 2012; Stieha, 2010). Disconnections are inevitable in learning relationships. Thus, the goal for the teacher or teacher educator is to learn to recognize disconnections and create opportunities for repair. The process of repair in learning relationships strengthens both teachers' and learners' capacity to learn and grow.

Just as disconnection can be understood as a form of resistance, repair can be understood as a form of resilience. In contrast to understandings of resilience as an individualistic move, a relational view of resilience is understood as a process of movement including "*supported vulnerability,*" "*mutual empathic involvement* in the well-being of each person and of the relationship itself," "*relational confidence,*" shifting from "'power over' dynamics to *empowerment,*" and moving toward "creating meaning in a more expansive *relational awareness*" (Jordan, 2004, p. 32, italics in original). By seeing resilience in this way, disconnections can be understood as moments of vulnerability that are mutually recognized by an "other" and where movement is made toward reconnection. Such action can lead to empowerment and strength. In the act of repair, relational awareness grows, and the relationship develops and is strengthened through the actions taken to reconnect. As teacher educators develop relational awareness and build capacity to detect disconnections and facilitate repair, they are also building capacity to support the learning of the teachers in their settings.

IMAGES OF CONNECTIONS AND DISCONNECTIONS

Research from our summer seminars helps to illuminate four types of connections and disconnections that may occur in professional development settings—connections with/disconnections from peer learning partners, facilitators (teacher educators), self, and the texts (or subject matter). Connections and disconnections may also occur with the context or environment, and Chapter 1 briefly discusses those dynamics. Using the relational triangle as a model through which to view the partnerships, it is possible to see the variety of learning relationships that coexist in an RLC (see Figure 2.1).

Figure 2.1. Learning Relationships within a Relational Learning Community

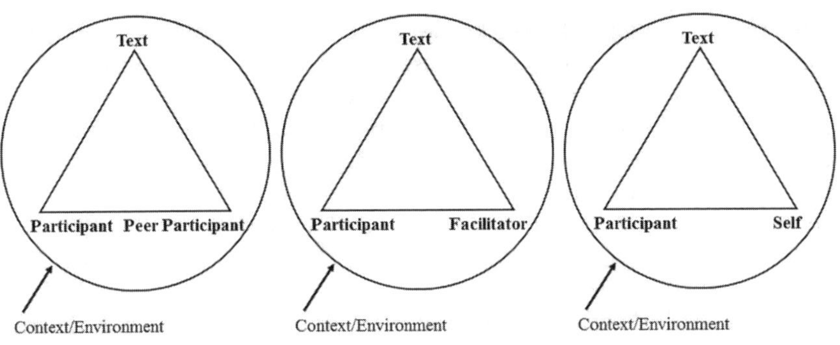

In the following section, I will explore the types of connections and disconnections that can occur within each of these relationships, and offer strategies that teacher educators can use to help detect disconnections and make efforts toward repair. The learning practices that can help build an RLC are the same ones that can elicit disconnections because such practices evoke multiple perspectives; supporting, challenging, and voicing actions; and efforts to yield complex understandings rather than superficial unanimity (see Chapter 4). The actions can stir up participants' worldviews, as well as their personal, professional, and cultural identities, often leading to a sense of disequilibrium. This disquieted or destabilized state can be a source of disconnection from self, others, facilitators, and texts as old understandings are relinquished and new ones are constructed. Of course, we do not seek to create disconnections in RLCs, but we must be alert to the possibility of their occurrence.

I begin with some images of connection and disconnection that the participants in our seminars shared with us. The images and metaphors are important and instructive because they help us, as teacher educators, not only to *understand* the relational dynamics that can occur but also to *feel* the depth and complexity of the experience as a whole. Connections were described as "unlocking," "complement," "flowing foundation," "looking through a different lens," and "connect the dots." These metaphors, actions, and images help paint a picture of how connections in a learning setting can feel, especially for the opening up of space, perspective, and flow of thinking. The images of disconnection that participants offer are similarly descriptive—"shut down," "barrier," "wall," "disequilibrium," "closed my mind," "broken link," and "hiccup." These images convey a sense of blockage, or closing of energy and space—the collapsing expanse that can jeopardize learning. With these images in mind, we turn our attention to the participants' descriptions of connection and disconnection in all dimensions of the relational triangle.

Connections and Disconnections with Learning Partners

A core relational-cultural pedagogy in our seminars was that of hevruta text study. While this pedagogy will be discussed in depth in Chapter 3, a brief introduction here is important for the following discussion. With ancient origins, hevruta text study is a Jewish approach to the study of biblical and rabbinic texts, traditionally occurring in dyads (Holzer with Kent, 2013). We selected this pedagogy because it offered participants the opportunity to experience a Jewish cultural tradition as well as engage in relational experience that proved pivotal in their learning. Through a pre-seminar assignment that asked them to describe their learning dispositions and experience with hevruta text study, we assigned the participants to hevruta partnerships that lasted throughout the entire seminar.

When participants described their sense of connection with their learning partners, especially their hevruta partners, they explained how "feeling connected" stemmed from different sources. Some felt connected by their similarities with their partners, while others enjoyed the intellectual challenge that stemmed from their differences. For example, Marie [2009], a language arts teacher at a Catholic middle school, reflected on the comfort of having a partner very similar to her.

> I was amazed over and over at the similarity between my partner (Megan) and me. We would consistently hone in on the same points. We often had to force ourselves to find meaningful challenges because our thinking was so similar. It was a very comfortable way to learn.

Marie clearly enjoyed the comfort of her compatibility with Megan and recognized the conscious effort they needed to make in order to sufficiently challenge one another. In contrast, Cathy, an English teacher at an urban high school, enjoyed the connection that she and Frank experienced that emerged through the sharing of their differing perspectives.

> [Frank], my hevruta partner, was a delight; he had the knack of asking questions that were very different from the ones in my mind, and I found his perspective and approach helpful in unlocking difficult texts. We seemed to complement one another through our different backgrounds and ways of thinking and also through our shared passion for helping our students grow.

The sense of productivity that emerged from their different worldviews and perspectives was a source of pleasure for Cathy. She also recognized that what they shared—their passion for student growth—opened up possibilities of connection as well. Similarly, Martina [2010], an administrator at a Jewish educational agency, identified the benefits of sharing similarities and differences with her partner:

> From the moment we read one another's pre-course writing assignment, we knew we would be well suited to learn together! We were struck by our many similarities, but also respectful of our differences that enabled us to support one another and push the other (and ourselves) to new levels.

Another way participants described connections stemmed from the ways that they could help each other grow. Using the metaphor of a "flowing fountain," Sarah [2007], a Judaic studies teacher at a Jewish day school, helped us see how this dynamic unfolded.

> With Jane, we would sit there and I would become [a flowing fountain]. I mean, I would just come up with ideas one after the other, like this. She took the idea, she was very smart, she would compliment, she would say "Whoa, that's a great idea." Great idea, and she can fly with it.

In this narrative, we can perceive how being heard and seen by her partner offered Sarah the opportunity to flow, and for them to fly. A sense of movement and energy is palpable. This description helps us see how the intellectual building between learning partners is an important source of connection in an RLC.

When adults learn together in an RLC, it is also likely that they will experience momentary or more extended disconnections from their learning partners. An innocent comment, or a comment made in a moment of frustration, could be felt as lacking in sensitivity, attunement, or understanding. For example, Hope [2010], a Chinese language and literature teacher for whom English was a second language, wrote about such a moment in a reflection after the first day of the seminar. She was describing a "speed dating" exercise that we facilitated to both examine the film *The Tribe* (2005) and to help participants get to know one another.

> When discussing the movie *The Tribe*,[1] when it comes to the last question, my partner (also my hevruta partner) says that he was kind of looking forward to talking to [Frank, another participant in the seminar] [about the movie]. I felt that maybe we have talked too many times for today and both of [us] needed a break from each other.

In this reflection, we can see her worry that her hevruta partner, Brad, had tired of her. This may have been an incidental or insensitive comment on Brad's part, expressing interest in Frank's point of view on the movie. While we cannot know what was in Hope's or Brad's mind during this exchange, it reminds us that the possibility of disconnection is always present, even if the reasons are not clear or self-evident. This reflection helps illuminate how passing comments might be taken to heart and prompt a disconnection.

At other times, different worldviews can lead to interpersonal disconnections. For example, Shira [2009], a rabbinical student, describes an episode of disconnection with her hevruta partner, Corinne, as the two of them studied the biblical Book of Jonah as part of their final project for the seminar. Shira explained:

> When [Corinne] and I were discussing the Book of Jonah from a literary or historical point of view, I felt absolutely comfortable. I was interested, engaged, and inquisitive. However, when she began to explicate details of her theology of sin and death, and later on when she was explaining why she thought the Bible was literal and why evolution never happened, I started to shut down. I felt very distanced and became extremely quiet. Coming from a very liberal California background, I had never before met anyone in person with her beliefs, and I was shocked by her words and the casual manner in which she stated them, sitting around my dining room table.

Shira, a Reform rabbinical student and Corinne, an urban elementary public school teacher who described herself as an evangelical Christian, confronted a difficult challenge in their hevruta work. They had experienced one another as comfortable learning partners until their theological philosophies were uncovered. Shira's disconnections—reflected in expressions and phrases like "shut down" and "felt very distanced and became extremely quiet"—are vivid. Corrine also described this encounter, but she did not experience it as a moment of shutting down, but rather as a learning one:

> I've always taken everything literally, like, okay—Jonah actually happened because he was a prophet and God sent him to warn Nineveh. . . . I knew the story . . . so when [Shira] said its allegorical . . . I was like . . . "No, Jonah lived."

In this interaction, we can see that the disconnection between these two learners was triggered by a text and their theological and hermeneutic stances, not by personality issues or learning styles.

Other times, the disconnections were more rooted in personality differences between participants. For example, Nancy [2007], a middle school social studies teacher at a Jewish day school, experienced intense discomfort with her partner, Anna:

> To sit down with my hevruta partner and for her to say to me, right at the beginning, "I don't talk. I just listen." [pause] . . . how do I bounce

> ideas off of you? . . . I'm not going to put all of the blame on her, but it just kind of put a barrier there and made it difficult to get through that barrier.

Because Nancy was someone who processed her thinking by talking and Anna did so by listening, these differences made for an uneasy relationship. Nancy eloquently explained the dynamics of relationship that created "that barrier"—an image of total disconnection—between her and her hevruta partner.

Connections and Disconnections with Facilitators

Connection with the facilitators or teacher educators is an important dimension of relational awareness. The nature of connections and disconnections between teachers and children (Chu, 2014; Raider-Roth, 2005a; Reichert & Hawley, 2014; Schultz, 2003) and in higher education settings (Murray, 2005; Schwartz & Holloway, 2012) has begun to receive scholarly attention. How the teacher-student relationship shapes the learning of an adult learner, especially in the professional development setting, is a newer area of scholarship—one that this book seeks to address. When thinking about how facilitators connect with participants, we must consider connections both with individuals as well as the group as a whole. Deborah [2007], a rabbinical student, commented on the public nature of the seminar facilitators' work, and how this helped her form connections with them and with herself:

> [The facilitators'] ability, especially, to open themselves up on a personal level through modeling. The use of song and on-the-spot sikkum writing. Their bravery helped me feel comfortable and allowed me to be more open and take more risks.

The sense of risk-taking offered a bridge of connection to the facilitators—sensing that the facilitators were "open" and invited her to be more open as well. Sally [2007], a language arts teacher and administrator at a Jewish day school, focused on the facilitators' connections with and responsiveness to the group. In responding to a prompt in the end-of-seminar evaluation asking about the aspects of the seminar that supported her learning, Sally wrote, "Having instructors who stay involved, inquire, and facilitate positive changes when needed." By highlighting the involvement, inquiry, and facilitation of positive change, Sally is reflecting on teacher educators' work of staying in-tune or attuned to the pulse of the group.

The disruption in relationship between the facilitators/teacher educators and participants is essential to recognize, for it is the one relationship in the triangle that we as teacher educators can act upon toward reparation with immediacy. The tricky part is that sometimes participants may be reticent to tell a facilitator about their sense of disconnection for fear of offending. Sally [2007] recounted a significant disconnection with one of the facilitators in her post-seminar interview.[2] In discussing texts[3] about the Jewish community's response to slavery during the Civil War period, Sally recounted her reaction to one of the guest facilitators of the seminar:

> There were two instances where he was talking about political reasons, political motivation, and he made a connection with his audience in an aside sort of a way, like, "You and I understand this—well, of course the Christians wanted [slavery]."

She understood this as a move to connect with the Jewish members of the group, and surmised that the facilitator forgot that some of the members were not Jewish. She recalls sharing her discomfort with another facilitator, but not with the guest directly:

> I lifted it up, politely . . . and I hope professionally . . . but I myself as a learner . . . when I lose faith in your intellectual integrity, I can't listen anymore. . . . It's clear [he] is a very learned man. He knows a lot of stuff. But because of the way I'm wired I wasn't, I was no longer positioned to learn from him.

While Sally did not lose connection with herself over the breach with this facilitator, we can see the disruption in her learning. One thing that is striking here is that while the facilitator's comment was likely an unintentional slip without intention to offend, it nevertheless was deeply hurtful and had potent consequences.

This consequence of a momentary teaching move leading to a disconnection was also captured in Norma's [2009] reflections. Feeling self-conscious about being one of the few participants who did not graduate from college, Norma (a teacher at a Jewish religious school) was highly self-reflective about feeling that she read the texts differently from others. She referred to herself as a "fish out of water" in this seminar, both in her end-of-course reflection and in her post-seminar interview. With this backdrop, she recounts feeling unseen by one of the facilitators. She commented:

> And I looked at it different, I guess, than everybody else did, and I could tell when we were discussing it and I raised my hand a few times because I really did enjoy that. . . . I think [he]—I could tell by what I was saying that he . . . it wasn't right or something. It wasn't where he wanted to go . . . where he was headed. So I thought, "Aw, maybe you've got to read that over again," because maybe I didn't read it right, or just saw it different, different view of what was it about, you know.

What is striking about this narrative is that Norma immediately reacted to the facilitator's response to her with the feeling that perhaps she did not get it, rather than feeling misunderstood. While many of us can recount times where professors' responses gave us a sense that we were wrong, Norma's honest and self-reflective comments help us see the potential consequences of a momentary lack of teacher presence.

Connections and Disconnections with Self

What do learners' disconnections with self look like? This may well be the most elusive aspect of the learning process to detect. We all have internal dialogues about how we perceive ourselves and how we think we are viewed by others—our strengths, vulnerabilities, fears, and capacities. Sonia [2009], a principal of a Jewish religious school and an artist, explains vividly how issues in her "own head" were barriers to learning:

> All of my stuff that were barriers were in my own head and it had to do with me. It was the physical issue and it was coming in as a lay teacher when everybody else was a certified teacher, so I was thinking . . . I wasn't worried about the Talmud study. I was worried about . . . "Wait, do I have the knowledge base or the skills that will match this group of people that I'm with when I've just been, you know, I'm a lay teacher?"[4] I'm doing the best that I can by instinct, by watching other people, by reading, but I've never been formally trained as a teacher. I'm . . . an artist.

Sonia described that what got in the way of her learning were her own concerns about whether her ways of knowing would be valued by the group. She realized that "I was stereotyping my own self." As facilitators, we did not learn of this source of disconnection for Sonia until we interviewed her 6 months later.

Sarah [2007] also articulately shared with us images and experiences of disconnection with self. Reacting to the multiple opportunities and requests for reflection during the seminar, she expressed sincere discomfort with these moments:

> When it came to do some kind of reflection on this . . . I was like . . . it was like a shortage. Like all of the sudden, a link, I have the link, and I selected links, I can give you a hundred, but there's a broken link here. . . . I'm missing something. And I feel it, that this is happening in my head. Some place in my head. . . . It's like making a pudding and it's not congealing. I have all the ingredients, I have good ingredients, from scratch, and at the end—where is it? And yet, I know.

Sarah's images of disconnection with self—her use of the idiomatic phrases "shortage," "broken link," and "pudding and it's not congealing"—are vivid representations of her emotional experience of these moments. What is most striking to me in reading this, as a teacher educator, is that we provided moments of reflection in order to create opportunities for *connection* with self during the seminar. And yet for Sarah, our intentions actually led to moments of falling out of relationship with herself.

Connections and Disconnection with Texts

When we consider the text as a third partner in the relational learning triangle, we understand that it has the power with which to form connections and disconnections. As I will discuss in greater detail in Chapter 5, we offered the participants an expansive notion of text, to include physical spaces, artwork, film, rabbinic texts, and archival documents. The synergy between these texts and the links that the participants made between them proved to be central to how they described their learning about Jewish culture.

As teacher educators, we often consider the ease of access and the possibilities that a text might offer to our participants in our workshops and seminars. The question is whether we also attend to the emotional and cultural dimensions of the participants' engagement with texts. For example, Lisa [2010], a curriculum coordinator at a charter school, reflected on the "place as text" dimension of the seminar, which included a daylong field trip to different sites of Jewish historical significance in Cincinnati, including historic cemeteries, landmark synagogues and temples, and historic and contemporary community centers:

> Both trips, the play, and the cemeteries were great. . . . I really enjoyed the Plum Street Temple. It was nice to connect to my own heritage and sometimes how much we all do have in common.

The Plum Street Temple is built in the style of the great western European synagogues of the 19th century, with echoes of the architecture of a cathedral. For Lisa, a non-Jewish participant, visiting and studying the Plum Street Temple firsthand provided points of connection between her own heritage and American Jewish culture. The sense of commonality helped her build a bridge to this particular text.

Disconnections with texts can be experienced on a spectrum from a small "hiccup" to immense interruptions. For example, Abena [2010], a middle school teacher at an independent school, wrote:

> I suffered a slight hiccup during the "I, Thou, It"[5] segment initially. I was extremely unclear about the text!! However, after we peeled it back [in the] whole group, it was very clear!!

It was interesting that others used the term "hiccup" to describe minor disconnections that were easily reparable. The image of a hiccup, as a momentary loss of breath, is an apt illustration of what loss of connection can feel like. Abena also astutely describes how the group (using the descriptive process described in Chapter 3) helped her reconnect with the article and find clarity.

Nancy [2007] offers us a very clear description of what a significant disconnection with a text feels like. For her, as a veteran teacher accustomed to textbook-like materials, the Talmudic texts presented a substantial challenge:

> But why I couldn't understand the material, was what really frustrated me. When it was coming to understanding the Judaics text, you know when it was written in Hebrew and then there was another transliteration, and then there was something else. You know, I, I just didn't understand how that all flowed together. . . . I'm sure [it] comes from the fact that, open a textbook, and there is. Okay. You don't have to go, "Well, this person says this, and this person says this," and then you have to come up with a conclusion. It's difficult for me [to] look at something like that. And especially when it's not something I was very used to.

Most poignantly, in reflecting on how she internalized this frustration, she commented, "I felt worthless, I really did." The intensity of this emotion reveals the high stakes of disconnection—a waning sense of self-worth. This consequence of disconnection helps illuminate why it is so essential to create strategies to detect disconnection and facilitate repair.

STRATEGIES TO DETECT DISCONNECTION

An important backdrop to developing the kind of relational awareness—the kind that supports being able to detect disconnection in an RLC—is creating a shared understanding with participants about the rupture and repair cycle. For example, by introducing the relational triangle (Hawkins, 1974/2002: Raider-Roth & Holzer, 2009; see Chapter 1) as a model for the teaching/learning relationship at the outset of professional development (PD) experiences, facilitators can make the relational dynamics between and among all the partners an "it"—or subject matter—to reflect on and discuss. Rather than casting connections and disconnections as personal issues, they can become part of the content of the PD work. Being careful not to let it overshadow the larger goals of the seminar, such as the focal culture being studied, relational reflection is an important dimension in detecting breaks in relationship, so that repair can be facilitated and deep learning can be cultivated.

After our first summer seminar, the faculty understood the need for intentional strategies to detect participants' disconnections. We felt it was important to have structured opportunities through which participants could both reflect on their sense of connectedness to the RLC and themselves as well as share with us where the threads of connections felt strong and where they felt threads were fraying. To begin, we added a question to our pre-course assignment (see Chapter 3 for a detailed description of this assignment) asking participants to reflect on ways that they cope during moments they feel disconnected from their learning (see Figure 2.2). By asking questions about what causes them to shut down or offends or distances them, we alerted participants that breaks in relationship or connection can be part of the learning process. This was important because often participants (and many learners in general) can experience a "shutdown" as a terminal event in their learning process—feeling that they want to flee. By introducing the idea that shutting down or disconnecting may happen, we hoped that participants might be better able to sit with the inevitable discomfort in these moments. In addition, by reading about the participants' tendencies when facing moments of disconnection, and their strategies for reconnection, we were able to watch for evidence of these moves so that we could be alert to moments of rupture and repair.

In a similar vein, we offered reflective opportunities at the end of each day, asking participants to consider their learning during the events and interactions of the day and comment on their experiences (see Figure 2.3).

The faculty read the responses each evening in an effort to understand both the ways in which relationships were being facilitated and ways in which connections were vulnerable and needed close attention.

Finally, we took seriously our associations, reading of body language, and hallway conversations that occurred. Often a casual conversation during a coffee break offered an opportunity for participants to share with us things

Figure 2.2. Pre-Course Assignment Question About Disconnection

Think of yourself as a learner and a teacher: What do you do when circumstances cause you to "shut down"? When something in a text or with a learning partner either offends you or distances you, how do you react? What helps you reconnect after such moments?

Figure 2.3. End-of-Day Reflection

1. Please describe one or more experience(s) or moment(s) from today that helped or supported your learning.
2. Please describe one or more experience(s) or moment(s) from today that hindered or interrupted your learning.
3. Please tell us if there is anything on your mind that you would like us to know.

they might not have said in the full group or even in writing on the reflection pages. We added these comments to the fieldnotes of the day, so that we could then talk about them as a faculty during our evening planning sessions.

STRATEGIES FOR REPAIR

As discussed earlier in this chapter, repair can be understood as acts or processes of resilience, in which people's inner strength can be evoked by speaking their minds, making their needs known, and seeing the effects of such communication. Relational resilience strengthens the relationship through acts of mutual responsiveness, careful listening, and attentive action.

In some ways detecting the breaks in relationship is simpler than repair, depending on the extent of the fracture. In our research (Raider-Roth et al., 2012) we found that if there was one break in the relational triangle, repair was possible to accomplish. However, if there was more than one break, or if the rupture was deep, repair was more difficult (see Figure 2.4). Sometimes repair required a great deal of guidance from the facilitators, and other times a group process was sufficient to rebuild connection.

Repair with Learning Partners

While we worked intensively to create hevruta partnerships that we hoped would be successful (based on the participants' pre-course assignments), there were times when the relationships did not flow smoothly. We tried to address these breaks in relationship when we were made aware of them

Figure 2.4. Breaks in the Relational Triangle

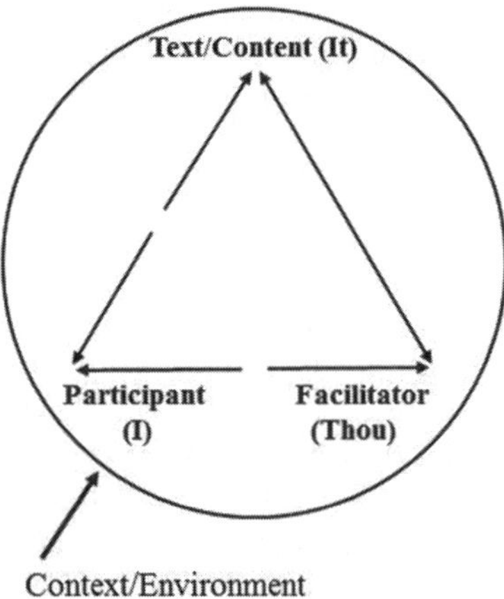

(through private conversation or daily reflections) or when we observed body language that suggested a lack of connection (such as long stretches of silence, looking at the text for extended periods of time rather than the partner, etc.). When the ruptures appeared to be minor, we were sometimes able to support repair through a response to daily reflections. For example, when Hope [2010] wrote about her concern that her partner had tired of talking with her, I wrote in the margins of her reflection sheet:

> Hope, it's worth checking with [Brad] about what he meant by this comment. It may not be about *you* but about wanting to get to know [Frank]. Also, in trying to understand different cultural meanings, it's important to try to understand where both of you are coming from. (Emphasis in original)

Hope had been open with the group that because she came from China and was bilingual, she was positioned in a more marginal state. My comments were meant to help Hope view this disconnection as an opportunity for learning about how dynamics of culture might have been mediating her relationship with Brad.

Other times, when the rupture was more substantial, such as when Nancy and Anna had trouble finding common ground in their shared text study, one of the facilitators sat with them, trying to help build a bridge of connection. Another day, we asked Sally, who was a colleague of Nancy's and had been paired with me as a hevruta partner, to join Nancy and Anna, to also offer other possibilities of connection. This was helpful for Nancy,

> because Sally helped pull our ideas together. . . . Sally just kept saying to her, "What are you talking about? . . . What are you talking about, tell me what you are talking about?" You know it helped.

Even in describing the repair, we can hear Nancy's frustration in not understanding Anna's meaning. Sally offered a temporary bridge but it was not a complete repair, as Nancy never felt that the relationship with Anna truly worked on its own.

Repair with Facilitators

Building on responses in daily reflections as well as faculty observations, we made conscious efforts to be attuned to moments of disconnection between ourselves and the participants. Sally's story of disconnection with the guest facilitator is one of the clearest examples from our research. It is also an example of incomplete repair. Sally shared her concern with another faculty member but never had the opportunity to share it with the guest scholar. Sally's experience speaks to the centrality of having consistent facilitators, rather than a common PD experience of guest speakers who "pop in" for an hour.

Minor ruptures were also detected in the daily reflections. For example, Frank [2010], a middle school social studies teacher at an independent school, wrote in response to the question about experiences or moments that hindered his learning:

> *Hinder* is a strong word, but I do find it slightly annoying when facilitators project their time management problems on the participants. And don't worry, you guys are not the first I've seen do it, nor the worst.

This was an important learning moment for us as facilitators, and we worked to separate our facilitation worries from the participants' learning. The next day, Frank wrote at the bottom of the page, "Random observation: Time management is much improved." What is important to me here is not that we improved our time management per se (though we were pleased he sensed our efforts in this regard), but that Frank felt his observations were taken seriously and acted upon. Shira wrote a similar observation in her end-of-course evaluation, when we asked about hindrances to her learning: "Can't actually think of anything . . . anything I wrote down in the daily sheets were corrected the next day!" Again, what is important here is her sense that ruptures were addressed in a responsive manner.

Repair with Self

Supporting a participant's repair with self is tricky because facilitators do not often know that the rupture has occurred. Part of our work as teacher educators, then, is to help participants become aware of their movement in and out of relationship with themselves. One strategy we used during the seminars to help participants tune into their own learning process was creating time during each day for participants to write in their journals (which were provided at the beginning of the seminar) about how they were experiencing the day, a group discussion, or a physical place. The facilitators did not read these journals, as the goal was to allow participants to keep a finger on their own pulse and the ways in which they could see their own learning. For example, Naomi [2007], an administrator at a Jewish day school, described how her journal helped her see herself and her own learning. During her follow-up interview she read to me from her journal:

> I had a revelation about myself and my learning style. I realized that much of the disequilibrium caused by experiential coursework is because I was never exposed to this kind of learning as a student. . . . It was so foreign to me, it was not the kind of learning I did when I

> was . . . I was a rote learner. I was a great student, but I never had to think.

In a sense, the facilitator's job in this respect was to provide opportunities for participants to detect breaks in relationship with themselves, to notice when they stop knowing what they know, when they experience self-doubt. This sort of journal writing must be purposefully supported, offering prompts, cues, and moments to which attention should be focused.

Daily reflections described earlier also served the purpose of (re)connecting with self. At the end of each day, we asked the participants to spend a few moments thinking about the day. In addition to providing feedback to us, as facilitators, so that we could be alert to the ways that the program was both supporting and interrupting learning, we hoped that the moments of quiet would allow for a touching base with self.

One practice that we also implemented each day was a collective reflection, or *sikkum*. Building on descriptive processes (Carini, 2001; Strieb, Carini, Kanevsky, & Wice, 2011), and a practice I had watched the eminent teacher educator Vito Perrone perform at the annual conferences of the North Dakota Study Group, I offered a sikkum or summary of each day, based on my observations of the day. (For a more complete background and purpose of the sikkum, see Chapter 1). I built on the notable experiences, humorous moments, significant learning moments, visible challenges, and oral collective reflections in which we engaged during different experiences of the day. The purpose of the sikkum was to make our learning visible and to bring together the many pieces of the day into an integrated whole. For example, in an excerpt of a sikkum midway through the 2010 seminar, I reflected on the mood that I detected—many participants were tired and beginning to think about how to bring their learning back home. The morning after the group watched a staged reading of Ives's (2010) play "New Jerusalem: The Interrogation of Baruch de Spinoza at Talmud Torah Congregation: Amsterdam, July 27, 1656," we began to draw together key themes of the seminar, such as emancipation, individual rights and group rights, and secularism. One methodology for doing this was through a descriptive process of the painting *Milton Visiting Galileo When a Prisoner of the Inquisition*, by the Jewish painter Solomon Alexander Hart (1806–1881). (This methodology will be discussed in detail in Chapter 3).

> We arrived this morning, full of thoughts, full of questions, a bit tired from our journey. We have many images, ideas, dates, faces, people. It's time to start organizing them, like photos, into an album, to see where we have been, and where we still need and want to go.
>
> So, we arranged the images from last night, from the Interrogation of Baruch De Spinoza. We shared our responses with one another, like laying out the photos on the table, seeing which goes with which.

We then began to organize the photos from the week, creating album pages for Abuyah, Spinoza, Mendelssohn, Solomon Alexander Hart. Premodern, traditional, Enlightenment, legal and civic emancipation, individual rights and group rights.

To begin the emancipation section, we described the painting, *Milton Visiting Galileo*, and we observed and looked, and noticed: books, a compass, a telescope, a lock on the door, hands clutching items, embers, light, eyes gazing right at us.

We raised questions:

- As a community where do you draw the line?
- How can Judaism be secular?
- Why such a focus on the outsider?
- What does it mean to expand the boundaries of what it means to be Jewish?

What meaning could we derive from looking in this way? Art visiting science. Is Galileo a martyr? Power of the monk, power of the church? New ideas about individual and group rights.

Our album work paused with a new page on reflection. What do we do when we are in a felt difficulty? Flee? React? Or reflect. To reflect means to observe, describe, analyze and take intelligent action. It all leads to another experience—and the possibility of a new felt difficulty.

After lunch, we returned to our work of listening. Of understanding the interpretive turn, the interpretive cycle.

And our discoveries were deep.

> "This procedure is directed at how we learn, opening up our mind. I sometimes forget about the process."

> "Makes you think, even if you don't want to. Help to make them better thinkers."

> "Teaches me to be patient and not close my mind off to the first thing I think of. Sometimes we get so busy that we stop hearing."

> "Not be afraid of an obscure text (it's not clear). You should allow yourself that they have the courage and respect and trust to see more than one possibility, and hold on to more than one possibility. To remain with ambiguity."

> "Mesmerized by the fact that in such a short space you can develop such a rich story. Each word in the text has its own meaning."

> "This kind of engagement with text has something we have to do with the kind of person we want to be."

> "Isn't all education pushing you to be a certain kind of human being?"

> "This story is about false pride and arrogance is blinding."
>
> "The choices that we make have serious consequences. If you absent yourself from relationships then you should expect some serious consequences."
>
> "Central to this is the whole ego."

Our day ends with pages in our album, some of the photos are organized. There are still many on the table. And tomorrow, camera and water bottles in hand, we will find new sites to observe, describe, analyze, and figure out how we will take action.

In composing this sikkum, I tried to weave together key themes and experiences from the day, as well as comments participants had made about their own learning. While I had not thought about the sikkum as a form of repair, some participants experienced it as such. Norma [2009] recounted:

> [The sikkum] put things in perspective . . . made me think about, what we had, you know, since we were in that moment, and [Miriam] was outside watching everybody and she was sort of in a different place, but when she . . . brought everything together and it made me just sort of kind of sit down, relax, and say, "Oh yeah, we did just do that."

It is Norma's comment of "brought everything together" that highlights one way the sikkum facilitated repair, with self, text, and the group.

And yet, as Sarah so eloquently shared with us, the moments of reflection that we offered the group could be experienced as disruptive as well. With Sarah's insights, we understood that peer learners were also important sources of repair with self.

She described her internal experience of reconnection:

> Yes, it also felt good because I felt that I had to offer, even to the advanced rabbinic students in a sense that, certainly my language background, but also because I grew up in Israel and my education was there, then I knew things and quotations, and I could put together things. . . . I could have references "this is what this says about this and this is about this" and that also made me feel good.

Her comment of "I could put together things" stands in sharp contrast to her sense of self as a "broken link" or "a pudding [that's] not congealing." In relationship with her hevruta partner, she had reconnected with self. Sarah's images and understandings shed important light on the ways in which the relational triangle is dynamic and fluid. The relationships rely on one another and shape and are shaped by the forces of connection and disconnection within the triarchic whole.

While Sarah offers a clearly rendered image of reconnection or repair facilitated by her hevruta partner (or in more general terms, her peer learner), Sonia helps us see the ways that the RLC itself can facilitate repair with self. As we saw above, Sonia struggled with her self-image in the group as a nontraditional teacher and as an artist.

> [As] you start talking and listen to what other people say, I would speak and nobody was like aghast that I was stupid. . . . I could feel like some things that I said were valuable . . . so that made me feel more confident, and, I was just honest about it. You know, this is based on my life experience. I'm not formally trained. . . . So, I gave myself a break part way in and, let that go, and it was a good experience.
>
> It was an incredibly supportive group. I think we all got the concept of exposing yourself and trusting and being able to be challenged but understanding that the challenge was for growth, not for knocking you down. So we were good at that. Which made it a pretty fertile environment in which to learn. I think that was . . . you just didn't need to feel isolated. We were a very encompassing group.

As we can hear in Sonia's narrative, the RLC created a "pretty fertile environment in which to learn." The core practices of voicing, supporting, and challenging are reflected in her comments of "exposing yourself and trusting" and "understanding that the challenge was for growth, not for knocking you down." Such an environment reduced the sense of isolation she and others feared and experienced when they first arrived. The RLC was "a very encompassing" group, thereby helping Sonia reconnect and see herself as a person with value: "some things that I said were valuable . . . so that made me feel more confident."

Repair with Text

This repair (I-It) is a tricky one because at first blush it can seem to be a one-way repair—how can the text initiate or participate in repairing a break in relationship? In these cases, a learning partner or facilitator might be needed to participate in the process of repair. As discussed earlier in the chapter, learners' disconnections with a text can be intrinsically linked to their life history and positionality that they bring to the relationship. For example, Sally [2007] shared that a text-oriented disconnection occurred for her when Elie taught a Hebrew liturgical song for the participants to sing each day. Not being a Hebrew speaker, Sally felt "othered," or outside of the experience. Watching her physical retreat, Elie offered a wordless option for singing that did not require a working knowledge of Hebrew. In this instance, modifying the text or offering multiple forms of engaging with the text provided an opportunity for reconnection.

Sometimes it is another text that can provide steps to reconnection. For example, Andrea [2010], a director of a Jewish religious school, commented that one session's discussion of a reading by the philosopher Spinoza was off-putting because she did not have enough background knowledge to understand the text. She found herself tuning out and not engaging in the discussion. Only later that evening when the participants viewed the staged reading of David Ives's (2010) play about Spinoza's trial for treason did she begin to feel that she could reconnect with the ideas and discussions. The live dramatic text offered entrée to the ideas that the printed reading did not.

DETECTING AND REPAIRING CULTURAL DISCONNECTIONS

This chapter began by unpacking the idea of relational awareness—including the detection of culturally induced disconnection as a form of social justice action. Thus far, we have looked at disconnections within and among the partners in the RLC. In a sense, learning to become alert to ruptures in immediate relationships is the best training ground for developing a sharpened relational awareness. By observing the current, live relationships that are more tangible, more at hand, we can experience the trial-and-error that is part and parcel of the rupture-repair cycle. With this increased awareness, we are better able to detect culturally oriented disruptions in teaching and learning relationships.

This sort of educational social justice practice for teacher educators is informed by the scholarship emerging from the world of counseling and social work. It is the perspectives on empathy that I think can be especially edifying for teacher educators. As discussed in Chapter 1, the affective and cognitive dimensions of empathy support our capacity to take others' perspectives, and as such are integral to democratic education. Segal (2011) builds on this understanding of empathy by connecting it with larger understandings of oppression, labeling this as "social empathy." She defines this concept as

> the conjunction of individual empathy and deep contextual understanding of inequalities and disparities. The combination of empathy and an informed understanding of the historical, social, and economic contexts of oppression can enhance the measurement of this concept and promote social responsibility while advancing social action and justice. (p. 268)

In culturally focused RLC work, understanding the "contexts of oppression" that influence the history and current life of the culture being studied must be a central dimension of the "it" or the subject matter. In this way, participants' understandings of oppression are evoked, and available for observation, description, and understanding. In a sense, these understandings are, in the words of Kegan (1994), made "object" rather than "subject." In the act of transforming an idea from subject to object, "we can 'have it' rather than 'be had' by it—this is the most powerful way I know to conceptualize the growth of the mind" (p. 34). By making object our understandings of oppression, we can build our relational awareness "on the personal and sociopolitical levels" (Comstock et al., 2008).

For example, Gwen [2010], a middle school teacher from a rural school, found the exposure to the diversity of Jewish experiences to be a "liberating experience." She commented:

> I was not aware of their experience. I [thought] that they were rigid in their religion. And that I needed to respect that and—which I still do. But so none of that's changed, it's just that I don't have this preconceived notion that they believe one way.

In letting go of these preconceived notions, Gwen spoke movingly about her sense of liberation:

> I felt like it was really . . . freeing and liberating for me because . . . I could free up some of the thoughts . . . that were maybe untruths or myths or legends or whatever. I could just be freed up to . . . think more openly and . . . not categorize or label or whatever, put people in a box. . . . It just had a bigger playing field. I had a bigger group of people to work with and there were no limits because of anything, any preconceived notion, or any prejudice or whatever might—anything I would have learned or been taught or thought was true or Hollywood-ized or—you know. All those kinds of things. I was just freed up.

Gwen's comments illuminate how unlearning stereotypes (all Jewish people "believe one way") led her to a sense of personal liberation, of being "freed up." She made deep connections between this sense of liberation to larger understandings of oppression.

> But all people have that experience of being oppressed at one time or another or left out or excluded. And at—certainly the Jewish experience is certainly one of them that is more—one of the more extremes of that . . . So in learning from that extreme experience also the continuation of that experience—in our world today. You know, I mean, it—to me, it's just—it's just—I don't know. Like kind—you—it kind of rocks your world when you think. . . . And you know, some of the things that you overhear students say. You know, and they're learning and, you know, I think—we—where we are right now, we think, "Oh, that is all behind us." Isn't that—I mean, "Nobody thinks like that anymore. Nobody talks like that anymore." But yeah, they do.

In this narrative, we can hear Gwen searching for words, trying to come to terms with the fact that oppression still exists in our culture—in her school, in the larger American culture. While it might be tempting to deny these kinds of oppression, the seminar helped her understand the "continuation of that experience." By learning about historical periods of anti-Semitism in the United States and Europe, Gwen made strong connections with other cultures/people's experiences of oppression. She recounted that she returned to school with "that sense that I had more than I thought I had to offer." She returned to school with a renewed sense of agency. When I asked her in an interview to explain this experience of agency, she replied:

> I have more connections with that experience than I ever realized. Well, like—I—relating to the civil rights connection. Relating it to any other oppressed people's connection. Or groups of people. I mean, even when I think of like my middle school lunch duty that I just came from, you know, where the 8th-grade girls are trying to divide each other up among—for their DC trip, their Washington, DC, trip. And—and they're trying to see who's going to room with who and who will be happy, and someone's getting hurt. Someone's getting excluded. And you know that's not okay.

Gwen's insight here is important, as the larger sociocultural learning offered her a new lens for the micro-relational dynamics occurring in her own school. With her own relational/cultural awareness increasing, her sense of empowerment to act as a teacher was enhanced.

SUMMARY

Developing relational awareness is essential for teacher educators and facilitators of RLCs. By building the capacity to detect participants' connections and disconnections with self, peers, facilitators, and texts, facilitators can keep a finger on the pulse of intellectual, emotional, and physical energy that is part and parcel of engagement with learning. In addition, such attunement can help facilitators support repair or reconnection processes when disconnections occur. Building relational awareness on the micro level (the ones inside the relational triangle) as well as on the macro level (the sociocultural pressures that can lead to a different yet significant form of disconnection) are critical processes for teacher educators. Such awareness supports the construction of robust and trustworthy knowledge.

Relational-Cultural Pedagogies

Hevruta Text Study, Descriptive Process, and Historiographic Inquiry

In constructing a relational learning community (RLC), the holding environment provides the necessary foundation for the hard work of learning—learning that can endure, and return with teachers back to their classrooms. Relational awareness is the core capacity to notice, feel, reflect, and respond to the dynamics of connection, disconnection, and repair that can happen as such learning takes place. This chapter takes the next step by describing pedagogies and practices that can support deep learning in the context of extended and in-depth professional development opportunities. In particular, hevruta text study, descriptive processes, and historiographic inquiry will be described. The concluding section discusses the notion of presence and the ways in which these pedagogies can support the development of presence in teaching and learning.

OVERVIEW

The pedagogies described in this chapter share five theoretical and pedagogical facets. First, each of these pedagogies holds the *relational triangle* at its core. As discussed in the Introduction, the relational triangle is a model that attends to the dynamics of relationship between and among the teacher educators, the participants, and the texts. In addition, this model includes the important role that the context of learning—the holding environment—plays in the teaching and learning process. Second, these pedagogies support participants' capacity to learn to be *present* to themselves, to one another, and to the texts (Raider-Roth & Holzer, 2009; Rodgers & Raider-Roth, 2006). Such presence is possible when each vertex of the relational triangle is activated and engaged. Third, each of these pedagogies involves practices that ask participants to learn to *look closely at the focal texts* of the professional development seminar. The act of looking, re-looking, or re-viewing was slow and careful work—not easy, sometimes frustrating or even boring—but it is central in the participants' learning. Fourth, and closely related to the preceding facet, is *slowing down* the interpretive process. By learning to attend or look closely, to pay attention to the vertices of the triangle, participants enact many practices before rendering judgment of a text or experience. Such slowing down invites multiple viewpoints to be shared, makes space for quieter voices in the group to articulate their views, and asks the participants to "not rush to judgment or conclude" before they have looked closely at the text (Carini, 2001). Finally, our research has taught us that these pedagogies are integral to the *transformative learning* experiences that many of the summer seminar participants reported. As Mezirow (2012) explains, transformative learning includes "becoming critically aware of one's own tacit assumptions and expectations and those of others and assessing their relevance for making an interpretation" (p. 74). Each pedagogy described below invites participants to examine their own assumptions as well as encounter those of their learning partners in the RLC. In this way, this work strengthens and continues to build the RLC.

These pedagogies and practices also exemplify the democratic stance that is foundational to an RLC. By widening the space of conversation, slowing down the interpretive process, and creating structured methods for diverse perspectives to be shared and questioned, these pedagogies embody democratic principles. In each practice, the participants and teacher educators need to attend closely to one another's points of view, trying to see the texts, relationships, and cultural context through the eyes of their learning partners. Thus, the practice of intellectual and affective empathy—a democratic cornerstone—is at the heart of this work. A central goal of these pedagogies and practices is that by "living" these experiences in professional development settings, participants can then bring them home, as a bridge toward enacting this stance in their classrooms.

HEVRUTA TEXT STUDY

A core pedagogy of our seminars was the teaching and learning of and in hevruta. When we first invited Elie Holzer, a rabbi and professor, to help us conceptualize and enact hevruta text study in our seminars, our goal had been to create an immersive cultural experience in which all participants could engage. Hevruta text study is defined as

> an ancient mode of Jewish learning, most commonly described as the study of traditional Jewish texts by a pair of learners. . . . It can be best conceptualized as the opening of a dialogue with a text together with a havruta [*sic*] partner. (Holzer with Kent, 2013, p. 1)[1]

In bringing hevruta text study to the seminars, we hoped to create an opportunity for the participants to build understandings of a Jewish approach to text study that involves questioning, multiple readings of the texts, and weighing merits of competing interpretations. The goal of this partnered learning was not to get the "right" answer, or practice debate skills, but rather to study a text in depth, offer possible interpretations, and support and challenge one another's interpretation with the goal of enhancing one another's learning. After the first seminar in 2007, we discovered that the curricularized approach to hevruta learning that Elie brought to the seminar (Holzer with Kent, 2013)[2] became a significant part of building and sustaining the RLC (Raider-Roth & Holzer, 2009; Raider-Roth et al., 2014). The reasons for this are numerous, including the sense of mutual responsibility this approach to learning brought to the group as well as the invitation to practice presence with learning partners. In addition, the processes of challenging, supporting, and voicing were core practices in the seminars' hevruta learning, and enacted core relational requirements for sustained adult growth and learning. These processes will be discussed in depth in Chapter 4. The following section will describe how hevruta text study was enacted during the seminars,[3] the preparation that was required, the texts we used, the types of pedagogical support that were necessary, and the participants' experience of responsibility and presence.

Preparation

Before the seminar began, we sent the participants a "pre-course assignment" that asked them to describe their dispositions as learners, their experience (if any) with hevruta text study, types of learning experiences that support their learning, and interactions that could cause them to shut down or disconnect. This assignment also introduced the stances involved in hevruta text study, and asked them to reflect on those stances that they thought would come easily to them, and those that might be more difficult (Holzer with Kent, 2013). We asked that the participants send these back to the faculty before the seminar began so that we could begin to "get to know" them. In addition, we read their responses carefully and used them to help us put the participants into hevruta partnerships in which they would study for the week. We undertook this pairing work carefully. While we sought to team up people with similar learning dispositions, we also sought to create dyads that were diverse culturally, professionally, or both. In 2007, when our cohort included teachers from a Jewish day school and rabbinical students, we tried to pair teachers with rabbinical students in an effort to have each offer a different expertise—one a pedagogical experience and the other content expertise. In addition, we tried to pair Jewish participants with non-Jewish ones (as a number of the day school teachers were not Jewish). In the subsequent seminars, when they were more diverse in terms of participants' religion, ethnicity, race and types of schools in which they taught, we tried to create culturally diverse pairs that were simpatico in learning approaches.

We did not know if using the pre-course assignment in this way would work in terms of creating strong learning partnerships, but we found that for the most part this was a successful approach. Martina [2010], an administrator at a Jewish educational agency, described her experience in her end-of-course response:

> From the moment we read one another's pre-course writing assignment, we knew we would be well suited to learn together! We were struck by our many similarities, but also respectful of our differences that enabled us to support one another and push the other (and ourselves) to new levels.

Martina's partner, Julie, a university faculty member, wrote an uncannily similar reflection (they both completed them at home following the seminar):

> As my partner and I silently read each other's pre-seminar assignments on the first day, we simultaneously looked up at each other and laughed. We couldn't believe how much we shared in common, even through that short piece of writing. At the same time, my partner brought different experiences and insights that enriched our experiences with each other and with our other partners, [and] the texts.

As we saw in Chapter 2, there were, of course, cases when the pairings were not as successful.

The Texts

During the first few days of each seminar, we used hevruta practices for the study of Talmudic texts that focused on the teaching/learning relationship.[4] Our goals were to support the teachers in both learning these text study practices as well as to study texts that could help them uncover important dimensions of the teaching/learning relationships.[5] For example, one central text, whose metaphor was often quoted during the seminars, was the first in our series of text studies:

> Rabbi Hama the son on Rabbi Hanina said: What is [the meaning of] what is written "iron sharpens iron?" To say to you: Just as [in the case of] iron, one sharpens its fellow. So too do two Torah scholars sharpen each other in Halakhah.[6] (Talmud: Tractate Ta'anite, 7a 11–14, brackets in the original translation)

The metaphor of "iron sharpens iron" simultaneously resonated, put off, evoked, and surprised the participants, and much discussion ensued about the meaning of this expression, what it meant in the partners' study experience, and its symbolism in Jewish tradition regarding text study. For those new to Jewish text study practices (Jewish and non-Jewish participants alike), the questioning/challenging stance conveyed in this metaphor was often unnerving. Questions regarding their own cultural and familial identities were called up—what was acceptable to their parents, clergy, and teachers regarding the act of questioning a sacred text, or the word of authority. These identity tensions will be discussed in depth in Chapter 6.

Pedagogical Structures

Many participants commented that they had experiences studying with partners or in hevruta before. What distinguished this hevruta experience from other forms of collaborative learning was that it was structured and curricularized. In response to the question asking what ideas were most important to his learning in the end-of-course reflection, Jake [2010], a middle school teacher at an urban public school, commented:

> Learning about the hevruta method of learning, i.e., the idea of learning with a partner, i.e., someone that will both support and challenge you to gain a deeper understanding. Sure, we often study with "partners," but having the structured sessions involved in hevruta make a big difference, I think.

He added:

> Having the time to work with a person one on one. Lately, this is something that I have not had the luxury of doing. And in a structured and allotted way. It is much different than a spontaneous studying/learning experience.

Joseph [2007], a rabbinical student, shared a similar reflection in his interview regarding his history with hevruta study:

> In rabbinic school they throw us into hevruta. . . . By the time I got to the seminar, I had already done hevruta study. Yet we never looked at . . . the methodologies behind that kind of study.

Shira [2009], another rabbinical student, agreed. She described her understanding of hevruta prior to the seminar: "This is Jewish tradition. This is hevruta. You study in partners. You're supposed to debate and answer questions. And that's what you do. And that was really it." She felt that the hevruta text study approach gave her "the tools to use hevruta in a new way—being able to say, 'All right, what does it mean to challenge someone?'

Because beforehand, in a class, if I'm in a Talmud study, 'I think it means this.' 'Oh, I agree.' 'Okay, great, let's move on.'"

What is striking in Jake's, Joseph's, and Shira's comments is the importance of the *structure* of the hevruta text study experience. While most adults have had experience with informal study groups, with pair/share experiences, or with some form of collaborative/cooperative learning group, the hevruta experience distinguished itself in the structured and curricularized nature of the work. For each learning session, there were particular practices on which to focus.

The curricular structure was rooted in two key stances—questioning and listening. Attentive questioning, as Elie Holzer phrased it during the seminars, asks the learner to look back at the text to help her figure out what the text is saying. It can also ask the hevruta partners to look back on their own statements to figure out their own ideas about the texts. Attentive listening is the sister stance to attentive questioning. "It involves intentionally focused attention and an openness to something that many not be easily grasped because of its elusiveness and complexity" (Holzer with Kent, 2013, pp. 107–108). Martina [2010] described her experience:

> My partner and I experienced how attentive questioning can "slow things down" for better observation. She asked a question about something that I had glossed over, assuming I understood the interpretation. Then we got to go back and find alternative interpretations, just by asking the question and slowing down the process.

The stance of attentive questioning and listening was the foundation for the practices of voicing, supporting, and challenging.[7] These practices will be discussed in detail in Chapter 4.

Ethical and Moral Responsibility

Attentive listening and questioning embody an essential ethical and moral stance. Hevruta text study offered the participants an immersive experience in taking responsibility for one another's learning. Holzer (with Kent, 2013) explains: "The ethical-relation aspect of havruta text study aims to have each student cultivate a learning relationship, a mode of being together which is *for* and *to* the benefit of his havruta partner's learning and growth" (p. 76, emphasis in original). Many participants were struck by this stance that we asked them to take. In a culture where "do you own work" is the norm, taking responsibility for another person's learning was often a new experience. As Tamar [2007], a humanities teacher at a Jewish day school, recounted:

> The unaccustomed sense of responsibility for another student's learning, which Elie emphasized in our first hevruta discussion, forced me to think simultaneously as a student and teacher. It caused me to slow down, to pay attention to my partner, and to think metacognitively about how I was learning the material and whether there were other ways to approach it. . . . So to stay with the same person and feel that responsibility towards what they know, isn't something I was ever asked to do as a student.

In Tamar's words, we can hear three central ideas. First, in assuming responsibility for her partner's learning she was taking on both the role of teacher and learner. Second, this "unaccustomed sense of responsibility" was a completely new encounter and not something that she had experienced before as a student. In a sense, it was redefining the role of student. Third, Tamar's understanding of responsibility hearkens back to Dewey's conception of this idea:

> One is held responsible in order that he may *become* responsible, that is, responsive to the needs and claims of others, to the obligations implicit in his position. . . . Being held accountable by others is, in every such instance, an important safeguard and directive force in growth (1932/1998, p. 352, emphasis in original)

The act of taking responsibility within the hevruta partnership is an experience that can shape the capacity to *become* responsible, to further one's own growth and that of others. Amy [2007], a primary grade language arts teacher at the same day school, commented about this sense of responsibility as well:

> How powerful the [hevruta] experience can be. The purpose is not simply to perform a task but to help each other grow, learn, and improve. The partners are responsible for one another's learning as well as their own.

Amy redefines the work of the "student." Rather than complete a task, which is a solitary experience, the work is to help another person grow. This is a radically different notion of student work. Hadassah [2007], a science teacher from the same school, also reflected on the responsibility she felt for her learning partner by describing both the work as well as the shifting of roles of teacher and student:

> I was challenged to listen to another person in an active way. I not only had to listen, but I had to help them to articulate their thinking.

> By my being able to ask clarifying questions to help my partner express her thinking I became teacher as well as student.

Hadassah's thinking highlights the fluidity of the teacher/student role as a central dimension of mutual responsibility. Our participants often recounted the fluidity of their roles. In studying about the I/Thou/It triangle (Hawkins, 1974/2002), the foundational model for the relational triangle, Cathy [2010], an urban high school English teacher, shared:

> If it is working, the triangle is constantly being reconstructed and challenged and reinvented and that process—that organic process—is what reminds me of one of my most favorite words in the whole article, which is *dignity*.

Following Cathy's thinking, the ethical and moral stance is linked with dignity, a fundamental aspect of democratic education. Such dignity acknowledges the humanity of both the individual and the hevruta partnerships. Liliana [2010], a humanities high school teacher at an independent school, explains this relationship eloquently:

> At the beginning we were not very comfortable because we didn't know each other. You may think that your partner may judge your intellect, but then, that fear disappears as long as you build a bond and are committed with your peer. You become who you really are.

Liliana highlights that as a person builds a bond with a peer, a fellow learner, the individual becomes "who you really are." Her comments underscore a foundational idea in relational learning—that growth is rooted in the *deepening* of relationships, rather than *separating* from the human connections that support us (Miller & Stiver, 1997; Raider-Roth, 2005a).

In a sense, the ethical and moral responsibility that develops in hevruta partnerships can be seen as an act of social justice. Martina [2010] explained it this way:

> One thing [my hevruta partner] said which I guess fits in here, that really struck me, was . . . we were talking about . . . texts and reading. And she said, again because of how she works professionally, she said, that for her reading is a social experience and it's tied to social justice. . . . And then the social justice piece of it was that it . . . in some ways it goes beyond just the two of us, but that's a way to sort of approach learners. That by giving people, encouraging people, . . . encouraging one another, sharpening one another, there's like a social justice piece of that too. Which I had never really thought about before and I thought that was pretty powerful.

Martina highlights that her learning with Julie, a university faculty member in the field of literacy, helped her see the act of interpretation as a form of social justice. With the multiple perspectives derived from the diversity of their partnership, they were able to support and challenge, encourage and sharpen.

DESCRIPTIVE PROCESS

A core pedagogy we integrated into the seminars was that of descriptive process. There are many origins of this pedagogy, stretching back to the work of Lucy Sprague Mitchell (Antler, 1987) and Carolyn Pratt (1948/1990) in the progressive teacher education movement of the early twentieth century. With roots in John Dewey's conception of reflection (Cuffaro, 1995; Dewey, 1910/1933; Himley & Carini, 2000; Rodgers, 2002), the practice of observation and description is a core dimension of reflective thought (Raider-Roth, 2011b). When encountering a "felt difficulty" in classroom life, a first step in addressing this discomfort can be observing and describing the phenomenon at hand. Taking this step back to see—larger, deeper, and wider—with the support of colleagues can help teachers consider all the possible ways they can respond to this disequilibrium. From the 1960s to the 1990s, Patricia Carini and colleagues brought descriptive process to the work of the Prospect School and the Prospect teacher education program (Carini, 2001; Himley & Carini, 2000; Rodgers, 2011). In this structure, descriptive processes were developed that could be shared with teachers across North America via Prospect Summer Institutes and later publications developed by the organization. These processes included focusing on describing children's work, children themselves, teachers' practices, and pressing issues in schools. In addition, other scholars were influenced by the structured nature of descriptive conversations focusing on children and teachers' work in schools (Abu El-Haj, 2003; Duckworth, 2001; Strieb et al., 2011), and new processes such as the Collaborative Assessment Conference were developed (Seidel, 1998). While different philosophies and practices concerning description have evolved, common to them all is enhancing teachers' capacity to see before rendering a judgment. Such a stance can support teachers' capacity to develop presence to themselves, to their colleagues and students, and to the subject matter (Raider-Roth, 2011b; Rodgers & Raider-Roth, 2006).

The collective practice of description is a decidedly democratic one. By inviting the voices of all participants in a learning community to articulate their observations from the vantage point in which they sit (literally and figuratively), the processes convey the importance of each member of the community. By slowing down the interpretive process to assist one another in collective vision, the community participates in taking responsibility for one another's learning. The recognition of the individual and the community is a humanizing practice, reminding us that learning is about opening our eyes widely and seeing what we thought we could not see.

In the seminars, we used descriptive practice to support teachers' capacities to see beyond their own "horizon" or point of view. As Jessica [2010], a counselor at a Jewish day school, recounted, "I truly fell in love with the idea of 'seeing' better and 'seeing' before I begin to develop my interpretations about a situation." Jim [2010], a psychology and sociology teacher at a suburban high school, agreed and considered his own teaching: "Using the descriptive pieces gave me a new perspective of how much I assume instead of asking what my students see for themselves." While we used these practices in 2007 and in 2009, we were most intentional and explicit about their use in 2010. By then, we had come to understand the centrality of their use in supporting transformative learning.

The Practices

The common practice in all descriptive processes is a disciplined observation of a given text. This means slowing down the interpretive process to begin by looking as closely and with as much detail as possible. In practice, this meant sitting in a tight circle and going around, one by one, describing one aspect of the artifact, document, or text. The aspect can be as focused as noticing the shading in a particular object in a painting. It can also be broad, such as noticing the medium in which the painting is rendered. In describing a written text, the "round" often was conducted by asking the first person in the circle to describe or paraphrase the first sentence or phrase. The goal is to stay close to the text itself, saying the phrase or sentence in one's own words. The next person in the round has the option of describing the next phrase or sentence, or going back to the first one to describe again, based on a different reading of the text. We learned early on that it was important to explain to the group that redescribing a phrase was not to produce criticism of the person who had shared the first description; rather, it was offering another vantage point on the text. We reminded the group often that our goal was to see a text from as many perspectives as possible.

When describing a film (such as a clip from a feature film, a documentary, or recording of classroom life), the work of description is harder, more closely resembling the work of observing or describing live action in a classroom. In this case, we asked the participants to take observational notes as carefully as possible. We suggested that they divide their paper into two columns, writing descriptive notes in the left column and questions/interpretations/judgments in the right. Even such a division on a page reminds them to distinguish between description and interpretation/judgment. We then viewed the film or film clip multiple times, allowing for the building of the observations and descriptions. In between each viewing, we asked the participants to comment on what they saw and the questions they had. Finally, after a carefully rendered description, we opened the discussion to what could be learned from the film.

We ended each observation/description exercise with a debriefing of what the participants felt they had learned. It was important to make their learning visible to them, as well as to us. For some participants, first encounters with descriptive processes can be frustrating—the participants sometimes reflected that it was "laborious," "overthinking," or "slow." We welcomed these comments, because they reflect a reality of the process. It is all these things. And yet such careful work opens up possibilities of seeing what they may not have experienced before. At these moments, we also made our teaching visible, explaining our purposes in using such slow and disciplined practices.

The Texts

We intentionally described many different types of texts. We began by describing a paragraph from David Hawkins's article on the I/Thou/It triangle (2002/1974), as a way to dig deeply into the triarchic relationship of self, other, and text. We described historical paintings such as *Milton Visiting Galileo When a Prisoner of the Inquisition* by the Jewish painter Solomon Alexander Hart (1847) and the Levy-Franks family portraits (18th century). We then described clips from films reflecting Jewish culture such as the prize-winning documentary *The Tribe* by Tiffany Shlain (2006); *The Frisco Kid* (Aldrich, 1979); Joachim Prinz's (1963) speech at the March on Washington; and Billie Holiday's performance of "Strange Fruit" (1939), written by Abel Meeropol (1937). Each one of these texts reflects important moments in or dimensions of American Jewish culture. A detailed discussion of our rationale for selecting these texts appears in Chapter 5.

HISTORIOGRAPHIC INQUIRY

The third pedagogical approach that we introduced in our seminars was that of historiographic inquiry. This approach was developed and led by the seminar co-creator and faculty member Mark Raider. As a historian, Mark brought this disciplinary perspective to our collective investigation of cultural texts. Distinct from hevruta text study, which derives its roots in Jewish educational-cultural traditions, and descriptive process, which stems from a phenomenological perspective on educational inquiry, this form of historiographical inquiry emanates from a disciplinary investigative stance. While its origins are distinct, this curricularization of historiographic inquiry shared interpretive practices with descriptive process and hevruta text study. The methodology invites a first reading, an associative reading, a skeptical reading, a contextual reading, and an action plan (Raider, 2010).

These readings, discussed in more detail below, also require an interpretive community, in which differing descriptions, associations, and questions can be shared. The collective nature of the inquiry embraces the democratic stance of the other pedagogies previously described. The richness of the descriptions, questions, and contrasting readings are dependent on hearing the ways these ideas resonate or clash with attentive colleagues. Similarly, by inviting "thick" descriptions, which is a profoundly intellectual endeavor, with associative thinking, which is a more affective form of thinking, the historiographic inquiry invites the "whole person" to engage deeply with the texts and their learning partners.

The Practices

Much like descriptive process, the first reading in historiographic inquiry asks the participants to name what they see in a historical document or text. It is a purposeful, slow reading of the text to help the community of inquiry see and illuminate as much richness and nuance in the text as possible. The second reading draws on the personal connections and associations that the individual brings to the text. What does this essay remind you of? What images, emotions, and memories come to mind? What are the lenses that you bring to viewing this text? The second reading is one of the distinctive features of Raider's historiographic approach. This dimension also occurs in hevruta study and sometimes in descriptive processes, particularly in "recollection" exercises (Strieb et al., 2011). In a description of the historiographic process included in the binder that participants received, Mark wrote, "What I seek to do at this juncture is provide the scope and inducement to let the text speak to us" (Raider, 2010). We can hear echoes of the relational triangle here, bringing the text into relationship with the reader and the community. This process reminds us that the text has a voice, it speaks to us. We need to make a space to listen and become aware of the ways that we respond to it. It is such awareness of self and other (in this case the text is the "other") that makes the associative process so important.

The third reading invites a skeptical, questioning stance. What questions come to mind when encountering this text? What is confusing, unclear, unsettling? This reading hearkens back to Dewey's notion of the "felt difficulty." With what aspects of the text do you, as a reader, find yourself wrestling? In a sense, this is where the seeds of inquiry are planted. The fourth reading asks the reader to bring the text to its historical context—era, setting, political environs, global events. This reading situates the process as a historical one and distinguishes it from the other pedagogies described above. It is an essential component in a professional development curriculum that focuses on the study of culture. Deep and nuanced understanding of the historical context of the texts is crucial for teachers as they build subject matter expertise of the cultural study.

After these careful readings, the final step of the process invites the participants to come up with an action plan—from the simple to complex, from concrete to more abstract. Mark (Raider, 2010) explains:

> All teachers know and recognize that real learning occurs when students take ownership of the materials they are studying and act on them in some way. Over the years, I have come to believe that action plans are essential to this process. In my classes, I ask students to develop action plans that sketch out what they wish to accomplish, the argument they seek to make, how they are going to use the materials and resources available to them, and what steps they need to take to realize their plan.

The action plan is a synthesis of the understandings, insights, questions, and new knowledge built in the first four steps of the process. It helps learners articulate their inquiry questions and integrate the insights, questions, and new knowledge constructed during the four steps into a coherent argument. It also assists them in sorting out the kinds of materials (such as various types of texts) and resources (such as tapping experts in the field—scholarly, witnesses of historical events) they will need. Finally, the action plan requires that learners construct a realistic plan to achieve the inquiry at hand.

Mark enacted this pedagogy in a number of ways during our seminars, particularly in the examination of historical documents, literature rooted in Jewish culture, and our field trips. For example, in preparing for the seminar in 2010, we asked the participants to read Kafka's *Metamorphosis* (1915), to introduce the notion of complexity of modern Jewish identity. During our first day of the seminar, we hung a long piece of butcher block paper on the wall divided in four rows (one for each of the first 4 readings). We then asked the participants to come together at the wall and fill in the rows, with thoughts, questions, comments, and so on (see Figure 3.1). We completed the exercise by reflecting on what each reading afforded us in terms of our understandings and then discussed the fifth step, the action plans people might take as a result of this inquiry.

In another instance, we visited the landmark Plum Street Temple, which Isaac Meyer Wise built in the style of the great European synagogues. We asked the participants these same questions, from which an intense discussion ensued about the associations that people bring to houses of worship. While some appreciated the ornate cathedral-like structure, others found it distancing and provocative. Participants found this approach to be both enlightening, practical, and eye-opening. Shira [2009] reflected on our visit to Plum Street Temple: "[The visit] made me jump out of my own feelings and think of how one text can have such opposite meanings for people and to be less judgmental in my words." Similarly, Teresa [2010], a high school

Figure 3.1. Historiographic Inquiry Chart

	Noticings
What stands out? Describe images, words, phrases.	
	Associations and Connections
What does this text remind you of? What images, emotions, memories come to mind?	
	Questions
What questions come to mind when encountering this text? What is confusing, unclear, unsettling?	
	Analysis and Context
How does this text connect with the historical context—era, setting, political environs, global events?	

language teacher at an independent school, reflected on the simplicity of the process and the depth of thinking that this process yielded: "The historiographic stance, great way of distancing oneself from the 'IT.' To deconstruct and to reconstruct something, to make sense of it. Understanding without judging, and then to proceed with the analysis. Simple and effective."

The historiographic inquiry process supported the participants' capacity to see the complexity of the texts we studied—written, oral, physical space, multimedia. This process invited multiple interpretations, an opportunity to understand one's own feelings and thoughts in order to step back to be able to hear and see the perceptions of others, and the capacity to understand without judgment.

A Concrete Bridge for Learning

For many participants, the historiographic process was simultaneously a learning moment and a concrete practice that they could imagine bringing back to their classrooms. It helped them think about ways that cultural texts could be introduced and unpacked collectively. Many commented about these dimensions in the daily reflections. For example, Abena [2010], a middle school teacher at an independent school, wrote:

> I *loved* the Kafka exercise. I have already started to draft a peer-share activity for my students using this and word problems. Great way to start the day. It acted as a mini icebreaker as well. (emphasis in original)

Other comments included, "I could see myself using this in the future" [Teresa, 2010], "I am excited to implement this in my middle school classroom during literature analysis" [Bev, 2010], and "It gave me ideas to begin my staff PD in this manner" [Lynn, 2010].

In addition to the applicability of the process, it is interesting to note that the participants noticed a relational aspect to the work. Like Abena's comment on the mini-icebreaker quality of it, or Lynn's comment about beginning her staff professional development in this way, the collective aspect of the inquiry stood out for the participants. In his interview, Brad [2010] expanded on this idea more extensively. As a novice social studies teacher, he reflected on the historiographic inquiry process:

> More than anything else that has stuck with me. I've used it in my classrooms several times. . . . I analyze text in my classroom without that and I analyze it with it and I noted . . . any differences there were as far as my students' comprehension of the text. And . . . based on my research and my data . . . it certainly helps with comprehension of texts. Mainly because with high school students . . . just taking it one step at a time, don't dive right into it.
>
> 'Cause that can really separate a group of learners. 'Cause one person can take the reins and go somewhere. Instead, [we] start slow and just describe what you see and then ask questions and then make those free associations and then not to step forward when you get into that analyses. That [is] really higher level thinking. By that time, because you started slow, you still have everyone with you.

In this narrative, Brad recounts a teacher research project in which he examined the process of studying texts with his students and comparing lessons that used the historiographic inquiry method and those that did not. In analyzing his data, he found that students had stronger comprehension of the texts using this method. He attributes this improvement to the slowing down, reining in, and not allowing one student to dominate the conversation. He reflects that the process helped "keep everyone with" him. It is interesting to note that a slower process, when one might worry about "losing" students, provided a structure for the group to stay engaged with one another and the text.

Liliana [2010] also noticed the link between the collective endeavor and critical thinking skills:

> The work done in class and in the archives gave me the basis of historiography. Being analytical and questioning the nature of the source helped me not to be judgmental and impulsive. I loved the idea of using visual sources such as the painting (which in fact I use a lot) but I never received training in observing so many details and then putting them together in [a] group.

In sum, the historiographic inquiry process invited a descriptive, observational stance that helped teachers bring back to their classrooms a rigorous, intellectual, collective learning process.

THE CENTRALITY OF PRESENCE IN RELATIONAL PEDAGOGIES

Core to the theory and enactment of hevruta text study, descriptive process, and historiographic inquiry is the awakening of *presence* in those who engage in their practices. My colleague Carol Rodgers and I have defined presence as

> a state of alert awareness, receptivity and connectedness to the mental, emotional and physical workings of both the individual and the group in the context of their learning environments and the ability to respond with a considered and compassionate best next step. (Rodgers & Raider-Roth, 2006, p. 266)

Presence is rooted in the relational triangle model. In order to build a stance of presence in teaching, it is essential to develop presence to self, others, subject matter, and the context in which one's teaching and learning resides. Presence is core to one's ability to develop relational awareness of self, others, and surroundings. It is this kind of awareness that distinguishes these pedagogies as ones that attend closely to the dynamics of relationship in the learning process.

We developed this understanding of these pedagogies as we studied our practice as teacher educators. After our 2007 seminar, when we interviewed the participants and studied their reflective writings, we understood that the learning partnerships of hevruta text study activated the three corners of the relational triangle (I/Thou/It) and consistently asked them to attend to themselves, their partners, and the texts at hand (Raider-Roth & Holzer, 2009). As a result, in our 2009 seminar, we highlighted this understanding in presenting the hevruta model. We explained the "inner logic" of our curriculum. We began by asking participants to be present to themselves, by doing the pre-course assignment and reflecting on their own dispositions as learners. We then asked them to become present to the text, by describing closely what they saw in the text itself. Finally, we asked them to become present to their learning partners, through the listening and questioning stance and the practices of voicing, challenging, and supporting. To reinforce these phases, we asked the participants to attend differently to the singing at each stage. When we first sang, we asked them to pay attention to their own reaction to singing publicly, the next day to listen closely to the sounds, and the 3rd day, walking while singing, to acknowledge the other in collective voice.[8]

Hadassah [2007] eloquently reflected on the connection between presence and the self, text, and other:

> I became more aware of my voice as a learner. I became more aware of my presence as a teacher. I gained a greater understanding of the significance of learning with a partner, and what that relationship stands for. I got a glimpse of text as a living organism to be connected with. My disposition as a learner and a teacher was gleaned. Cultivating the relationships in hevruta was so intense for me because I was able to be present throughout. I had a sense of value.

Haddasah's connection between presence and having a "sense of value" is crucial. The energy-filled language she uses to describe becoming "aware" of herself as a teacher, the "text as a living organism," and "cultivating the relationships" reflects a sense of agency. Such agency is connected to her sense of value.

This holistic sense of presence—as awakening the three corners of the relational triangle—was also evident in teachers' reflections on descriptive process. Jessica [2010] described the ways that presence was elicited in the work of descriptive process:

> The task [describing a paragraph from a text] was challenging, but I felt like it was a great way to review the text, be exposed to other people's perspectives, and re-evaluate my own conclusions.

By using descriptive process to slow down the interpretive process, broaden our abilities to see, and invite multiple ways of seeing into the learning community, we were also creating opportunities for teachers to hone their capacities to be present to themselves, one another, and the texts. In order to understand the ways that presence was built through these pedagogies, it is helpful look at each dimension of presence.

Presence to Self

Throughout the seminars, many participants also discussed the dimensions of presence in their learning. Rinat [2010], a preschool teacher, described how the hevruta work helped her become more present to herself and her own learning:

> My learning was supported in the way that its skeleton was made more visible to me. Or maybe I should say its neural paths. It started with the thinking and writing down ahead of the course, to fill the answers to the [pre-course assignment]. The intensity of the awareness when talking, listening to and thinking about issues such as the instructional triangle, sketching the steps that support good hevruta learning, . . . I have written and said dozens of times to my students' parents, to fellow teachers and to directors: "It's the process not the product!" And yet, I rarely examined my own process in a way beyond my level of involvement and (this mostly goes to creative learning) my feelings and enjoyment.

The learning experience of the seminar helped Rinat see her own learning "skeleton" or "neural paths." There was a sense of seeing herself that was new. She attributed this "intensity of awareness" to the "talking," "listening," and "thinking" that happened in the seminar.

Lynn [2010], a curriculum coordinator at a charter school, expressed a similar theme regarding her presence during the seminar:

> I think that . . . on a level of being present, I would—presence—a lot more during our seminar time than I had been, let's say in class. . . . Maybe it has to do with the facilitation of that . . . I felt . . . very productive and . . . alive during that week. Because there was so much to say and there was a great exchange of ideas that I haven't experienced . . . with others, either here at work or . . . in the past. . . . It's stimulating. . . . You know, in that respect, this was great because it was . . . a mutual exchange of ideas. It was respectful . . . and it was accepting. . . . Maybe we couldn't . . . come to agree on something, but that was okay.

This quote from Lynn's interview reveals her presence to herself and her learning—as expressed in her use of the terms "productive," "alive," and "stimulating," echoing Hadassah's energy-filled description. She attributed this to the facilitation as well as to the "mutual exchange of ideas" and "respect." She paints this in marked contrast to her own past and her current work situation.

Presence to self is also key in descriptive processes. One common response in the descriptive process "circle" is often, "Wow, I didn't see that." In multiple rounds of describing a photo, a piece of student work, or a film clip, participants become aware of an image, a color, or an action that they did not see upon first viewing. For example, when teaching the skill of observation and description, I often begin with a 90-second video excerpt of my son when he was 18 months old. Because there is only one "actor," participants are more able to focus on the "action" than they might be when watching a group of children. When observing his engagement with different toys, some participants are sure that he has crawled, while others are sure he has not. By engaging in this descriptive process with others, they become aware of their own capacities to see. In this way, they become more present to themselves.

In historiographic inquiry, presence to self is often awakened in the associative process. In this step, participants are asked to become aware of the ideas, emotions, memories, and thoughts that the historical text evokes. Such awareness offers the opportunity to understand the lenses that they are bringing to view the historical artifacts, and their attempt to disentangle their own interpretation from the voice of the text.

Presence to Others

These pedagogies also invite participants to become present to the "other"—to their learning partners in hevruta, and to their interpretive community in descriptive processes and historiographic inquiry.

Amy [2007] articulately describes this kind of presence:

> I found it fascinating because it really made a lot of sense and . . . not only do you bring your self, but somebody else brings themselves and when the two of you try to—or brings themselves—and then when the two of you try to meet as partners you've got to take that into consideration and . . . this interaction within a triangle, I just found it fascinating.

Reflecting on the relational triangle, Amy [2007] considers the meeting of "selves" in hevruta work and the "interaction" and "consideration" this requires. This recognition of the "other" is a powerful enactment of presence.

Megan [2009], a preschool teacher at a Jewish community center, returned to her classroom thinking about observing and describing her students, which she connected to the notion of presence. The recognition of her students through descriptive process supported her capacity to be present:

> The whole issue of [presence] I went back into preschool class, and here I am with 2-year-olds and I'm thinking of . . . at certain points in seminar it talked about how [presence] of . . . the initial documentation with . . . children . . . and the experience of early childhood and that was important to [me]. Learning . . . the very detailed . . . description process.

Megan reflects that the stance of observation (the initial documentation) and descriptive process can help her be present with her young students.

While the historiographic inquiry most supports the development of presence to self and text, its enactment in RLCs supports participants' development of presence to learning peers as well. Such support is enacted in each step of the process where participants become aware of one another's questions, associations, and analyses.

Presence to Texts

Finally, participants also talked about presence to the texts that we studied. Tamar [2007] explained:

> Another key idea I took from hevruta study was the "I-Thou-It" triangle composed of either the student, teacher, and text, or two hevruta partners and a text. The concept of the text being an equal partner, having a voice (although a fragile, easily overpowered one) was powerful for me. I very much wanted to give my students that sense of treating the text as a living voice, one to which they had to carefully and considerately listen.

As a middle school language arts teacher, Tamar thinks carefully about the place of narrative and text in her students' learning. Her learning about the text as a partner, as a vertex on the relational triangle, as an "other" with which a relationship could be developed, becomes quickly applied to her thinking as a teacher. She noted:

> Encouraging students to see the text as a partner struggling to say some specific thing, if only they are listening, seemed likely to be a metaphor that would lead them in promising directions.

Invoking the need for "listening," Tamar weaves together the practices of hevruta with the intention of helping her students learn to be present to the text. By ascribing human dimensions to the text as a "partner struggling to" speak, she highlights the capacity for building connection with the text.

As a sister practice to hevruta learning, descriptive process also invites participants to see the text as a living organism. By spending such focused time with the text as a third partner, they develop a new kind of relationship with the text itself. It becomes alive in a way that it had not prior to the act of describing.

Presence to text is the heart of historiographic inquiry. Akin to hevruta text study, the process begins with making space for the text to speak: What is the story told? Can we tell it without imposing our own associations? When we take the step to add our own associations, and cultivate our connections to the text, can our associations awaken dimensions of the text that we did not see when trying to remain "neutral" in telling the story? In these multiple readings of the text, the goal is for the historical story to come alive, and for us to become awake to its multiple tellings.

Presence and Context

In David Hawkins's original writing about the I, Thou, and It relationship, he did not attend to the dimension of context (or the circle that surrounds the triangle). Since the original publication of his essay, other scholars have added the dimension as essential to understanding the dynamics at play in the learning process (e.g., Ball & Forzani, 2007; Raider-Roth, 2005a; Rodgers, 2002; Rodgers & Raider-Roth, 2006). This notion of context can include anything and everything from the air quality, to the destructive "isms" in our culture (see Figure 3.2).

From a relational perspective, the nature of the learning context can exert strong forces to support or impede healthy learning relationships. For example, a scripted curriculum can make it difficult for a teacher to attend to the individual needs of students, since she may be required to "cover" particular materials in a given time span.

Figure 3.2. Relational Triangle Plus Context

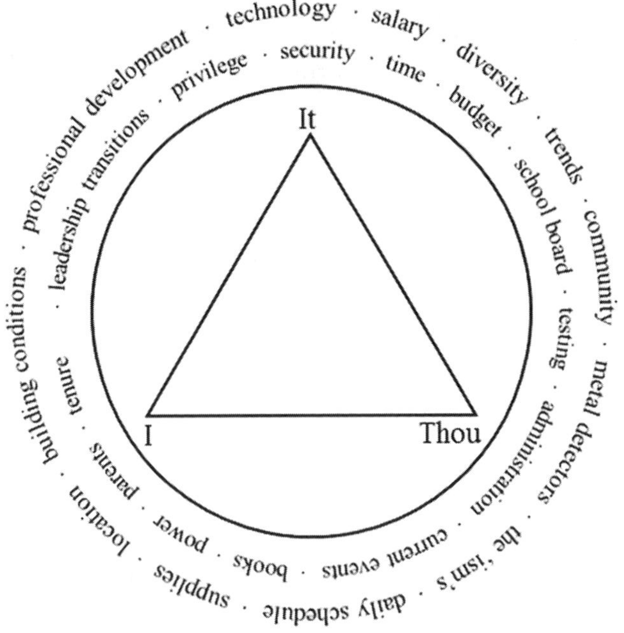

Source: Adapted from Raider-Roth, 2005a, p. 164.

In studying the ways that context shaped our participants' capacity to be present, my colleague Vicki Stieha and I (2012) examined the ways that a school context can support and thwart teachers' capacity to be present to themselves, their students, and the content. Based on Vicki's dissertation research, grounded in systems theory (2010), this study helped us see that a healthy relational school context (characterized by trust, mutual respect, and growth-fostering relationships) can help teachers cultivate presence. A school culture in which relational disconnections prevail can undermine presence. Thus, creating and nurturing healthy relational cultures in schools is a high-stakes goal.

SUMMARY

This chapter described the three central pedagogies that were implemented in the seminars: hevruta text study, descriptive process, and historiographic inquiry. The practices shared common underpinnings: structured practices that guided the observation; description, interpretation, and group process; supporting participants' capacity to observe more broadly and deeply; slowing down the interpretive process; slowing down the judgmental process; collective processes for unearthing multiple, varying, and often conflicting observations and interpretations; and assuming collective responsibility for one another's learning. These pedagogies and associated practices were fundamental to the construction of an RLC. As such, the practices lay the foundation for democratic learning opportunities.

CHAPTER 4

Supporting, Challenging, and Voicing

Why This Trio of Practices?

> We understand also that they [learners] are most likely to pose the questions with which learning begins when they feel themselves to be speaking to others, speaking in the first person to those who are different from themselves. When they can articulate what they have to say against the background of their own biographies, they may be in a position to listen to others—and be listened to—if those others are also speaking for themselves. (Greene, 1982, p. 7)

Learning begins when we pose genuine questions. Maxine Greene tells us that learning happens when we pose these questions in our own voices, facing our own biographies, to those who are different from ourselves. Such positioning allows us to listen and be listened to, if all learning partners are speaking for themselves. These are precisely the stances that we asked the participants in the seminars to assume. Assuming such a position is often uncomfortable—whether it is the act of facing our own biographies or "speaking in the first person to those who are different" from ourselves. To help teachers learn/strengthen these stances, it is important to provide them with abundant opportunities to practice, as well as offer and receive feedback from fellow learners.

What is it about these three practices—supporting, challenging, and voicing—that are particularly important? In this chapter, I will build on Robert Kegan's (1994) proposition that they hold the fundamental goals of adult development. He wrote, "People grow best where they continuously experience an ingenious blend of support and challenge. . . . The balance of support and challenge leads to vital engagement" (p. 42). Kegan theorizes that human growth is the result of achieving a dynamic state of equilibrium between just enough challenge and support. The goal is to push the adult learner to stretch, but not so far that she snaps. While Kegan does not specifically identify voicing in his original theoretical model, he implies this in his later work (Kegan & Lahey, 2001, 2009). I see voicing as a crucial component in this conceptualization. Voicing is the key act of articulating emerging ideas that can help a person achieve new insight and new ideas. In a sense, it is the articulation of the new understandings that can emerge in the challenging/supporting dance.

Our research over the past 10 years has indicated that in each of the seminars, these practices proved central in the participants' learning. We observed that these practices often placed the participants in a place of uncertainty, or felt difficulty (Dewey, 1910/1933), which led to new growth. In addition, they contributed to participants' sense of ability to author new ideas—a form of authority. Finally, these practices often provoked participants to revisit their identities, leading to new insights into teaching about culture, history, and society. In this way, these practices—which were offered and practiced as interpretive moves—had impact on the participants' sense of self as learners and teachers. This chapter will describe the practices of supporting, challenging, and voicing, as well as the kinds of learning that the participants described and we observed in the implementation of these practices.

SUPPORTING

The interpretive practice of supporting is key to assisting another person to take the necessary risks of uttering an insecure idea. A core goal of supporting is to help a partner extend and deepen the interpretation, to find more textual evidence to support the idea, and to locate and articulate the inner logic of the idea (Kent, 2013). Supporting practices were an integral part of the seminars' hevruta text study curriculum. They were particular moves that the participants took to help their learning partners extend or deepen their thinking. Supporting practices were more than acknowledging and complimenting a colleague's interpretation; they were demonstrating in some concrete form that her ideas were worthy of response and of being built upon. Just as parents might put a steadying hand on the back of their child who is learning to walk, the partner metaphorically offers a reassuring movement to help the other hold her train of thought. The dyadic practice of supporting—each partner offering the steadying hand to the other—transforms this practice to one that embodies mutuality and reciprocity. It is a move that requires action so that one's partner can take steps forward with her interpretation. When introducing the practice of supporting, we offered the following "moves":

- Look out for additional textual evidence to support the interpretation.
- Explain how this interpretation helps you better understand the meaning of this text.
- Explain what you like in this interpretation.

Paul [2009], a high school English teacher, eloquently described the anatomy of what mutual support can look like in hevruta with his partner, Sonia:

> She had the big idea and then I brought it into more of a concrete, a concrete form and pulled it all together . . . pull[ed] all of these different elements that we learned and then . . . explain[ed] it to the rest of the class. . . . I was sort of the interpreter. And she was the initiator. She came up with the idea and then I sort of put it into a form that everybody could understand. So we really, it, we really capitalized on our strengths that way.

Paul's description is replete with the dynamics of interpretation that he and his partner, Sonia, shared. She had the big idea and he was able to make it concrete. She was the initiator and he was the interpreter. Paul did not see these capacities in hierarchical form—that one was better than the other—but rather, they were complementary perspectives and skills. By identifying these complementary roles, we can hear the essence of mutuality in their support for one another. The give-and-take was not the same, but it was reciprocal.

Martina [2010], an administrator at a Jewish education agency, also astutely described the dynamics of her work with her partner, highlighting a reciprocity and mutuality in the work. She noted:

> As we shared different interpretations of the text (voicing, supporting, challenging) with different partners, I realized that it was not really about changing vs. keeping your interpretation—but rather to be able to see (explicitly) more ways of interpreting the same text. One of my new partners in this exercise and I were able to diagram the "choice points" in interpretation—the crossroads that could lead to different interpretations.

While Martina calls up the trio of practices, she explains one of the finer points of supporting practices—helping make explicit the evidence that buoys a given interpretation. Rather than trying to convince a partner that your interpretation is better or stronger, the goal of supporting practices is to surface the sources that could best strengthen a given interpretation. Such give-and-take, or reciprocity, in a learning partnership is an essential dimension of support in hevruta partnerships.

Liliana [2010], a humanities high school teacher at an independent school, added a core dimension of support—that of trust:

> Trusting and supporting each other is crucial towards the success of this practice. I like the exercise of support and challenge. I felt pleased with it because we were both equal and we were comfortable to doubt, to question, and to respect moments of silence and reflection.

In her incisive comments, Liliana teaches us that trusting and supporting are linked. They create an egalitarian relationship that invites comfort, doubt, questions, respect, silence, and reflection.

In sum, supporting practices enact core aspects of a healthy learning relationship, including mutuality, reciprocity, trust, and respect. Supporting is more than "being nice" or complimentary of another's interpretation; rather, it is a practice that helps hevruta partners build confidence in their interpretation. This kind of support must be substantive, based in textual evidence, and requires the enactment of attentive listening and questioning (Holzer with Kent, 2013).

CHALLENGING

The sister practice to supporting is that of challenging. Challenging asks the partners to help one another "better articulate and refine her own interpretation" (seminar notebook, 2009). Challenging is core to taking responsibility for each other's learning—not in the effort of "disproving" or tearing down of the other person, but rather in helping her build a more robust interpretation (Kent, 2013). In many cultures, challenging can sometimes be viewed as risky, aggressive, or impolite. Our view of challenging practices was expressly not aggressive, but rather in the service of helping one's partner move forward with her interpretation. In a sense, interpretive disagreement was invited and sanctioned, in the understanding that respectful disagreement had the capacity to open up a text and an interpretive discussion, rather than shut it down. It is this conception of challenging, I believe, that led to one of the clearest findings across our studies of the seminars: the importance of experiencing challenging during the seminars and bringing it home to the participants' classrooms, homes, and professional settings.

When we introduced the practice of challenging, we offered the following suggestions:

- Explain why you think an interpretation is not strong enough.
- Look for more evidence to support the interpretation.
- Share a piece of the text that seems to contradict the interpretation.
- Ask about an underlying assumption of the interpretation that does not seem to be represented in the text.

Elie also asked the participants to practice challenging their partners even if they agree with each other. "Challenging is something that you want to practice, obviously when you disagree, but even when you agree [with each other]." Participants were often surprised by this suggestion, and shared that this proposition extended the idea of challenging beyond their initial assumptions. This suggestion also reinforced the idea that challenging was about not only disagreement but also helping their partners stretch and take a step beyond their first thoughts.

By experiencing this curricular dimension of hevruta learning, the participants could practice these acts, which might have felt new, uncomfortable, or otherwise destabilizing. Many participants expressed discomfort with challenging moves, as unfamiliar or transgressive of the code of professionalism in their schools. A key discovery we made during the seminars was that the participants felt more comfortable enacting challenging practices because it was part of their *role* as hevruta partners and members of the relational learning community (RLC) (Raider-Roth et al., 2014). That is, deviating from (North American) cultural norms of being "polite" or "nice" felt risky, and being "required" to try out the practices in the seminar allowed the participants to "play" in their learning. We called this "role-sanctioned challenging" (Raider-Roth et al., 2014).

Amy [2007], a primary grade general studies teacher at a Jewish day school, commented on this aspect of what she called "permission":

> My experience has been when two or more adults get together to work on something. . . . We end up talking about our kids or mates, our gripes. And this didn't happen this time. And that is also why it was unique. We didn't get diverted. It's like we had a task, we understood what we were supposed to do, we did it together and it was *so* interesting that we really didn't need to digress, sorta avoid the task at hand.

Amy insightfully picks up on the diversion or digression that can happen when there is a difficult task put before us. She was fascinated by this phenomenon. When I asked her why she thought this happened, she replied:

> I didn't know [my hevruta partner] very well before this, and I just really value getting to know her better because . . . she has got a lot to say, she's a thinker and she's very specific sometimes, like, "Well, what do you mean by that," which is part of what you wanted us to do. Where I'm a little, I'm less, more tentative, I guess about challenging people's thinking. . . Knowing that she was doing that to me gave me permission within my value system to kinda do that back, it was going to be safe. If she could do it then I could do it. So I think that's what I meant. The one-on-one and sorta being given permission to be more assertive and more involved and knowing that she wasn't going to say, "well that's stupid," or "I don't agree with that.". . . That was . . . outside of the way you had painted it for us.

Amy describes important dimensions of role-sanctioned challenging: permission to be assertive and involved, the precondition of safety, and trust that ideas were not going to be denigrated (although allowing for disagreement was part of the role). I am particularly struck by the way that Amy highlights the importance of the mutual act of challenging—"knowing that she was doing that gave me permission within my value system to kinda do that back, it was going to be safe." While tentative about challenging others' thinking, Amy senses a safety in the mutuality of the challenging practices, and this connects deeply to her value system. That challenging was something that they were "supposed to do," as part of their roles as hevruta partners, added to a dimension of safety.

The idea of a "safe space" to be vulnerable was one that was described by many participants across the three seminars. Sonia [2009], a principal of a Jewish religious school and an artist, unpacked the idea of safe space in a quote we previously examined in Chapter 2 when discussing repair:

> It was an incredibly supportive group. I think we all got the concept of exposing yourself and trusting and being able to be challenged but understanding that the challenge was for growth, not for knocking you down. So we were good at that. Which made it a pretty fertile environment in which to learn.

Like Amy, she identifies the safe space and dimension of trust that was necessary for such challenging. In addition, the idea of "challenge for growth" not "knocking you down" reflects the kind of challenging we asked the participants to try. Most essentially, Sonia highlights that the sanctioned space for challenging also contributed to the construction of the RLC, a "fertile environment in which to learn." These ideas of safety resonate with those described in Chapter 1, when we discussed the roles of safety in building a holding environment for professional development. In this way we can see how the challenging practices are core to the building of a professional learning community.

In sum, a core dimension of professional development practices concerning the learning of culture is the construction of a framework that includes role-sanctioned challenging. That is, in studying cultural texts, artifacts, and spaces, learners must study in relationship with each other, challenging each other's observations, interpretations, and questions. In order to take the risks that this kind of work entails, it is helpful to build this practice into their roles as participants in the group.

VOICING

> Voicing is actually this idea where sometimes we feel inhibited to say what is an intuition that we begin to have. So we have a beginning of an idea, we're not sure about it, and we're not saying it because we want to be heard

> as knowing precisely what we know. Or sometimes we have an idea where it leads us to a place where, "Hmmm, would that be the idea that the text would have . . ." So we are silencing ourselves because we would prefer not to be identified with this idea. (Elie Holzer, video transcript, 7/28/09)

Voicing may begin in the *intrapersonal* space—in the internal conversations that a people may have with themselves. Not ready to yet say the idea aloud, the person may mull over, internally argue, or dialogue about the merits of a particular idea or interpretation.[8] This internal act of voicing, to allow one's own creative thinking process to occupy mental space and focus, requires courage. Yet many of us are masters of self-silencing and self-critique—the ways that the harsh self that Tim Gallwey (1974) calls "Self 1" or the "teller" talks to the Self 2, "the doer," in his classic book *The Inner Game of Tennis*. The process of bringing these internal voices or ideas outside of one's self can be a risky enterprise.

The risks of voicing, what Kegan and Lahey (2009) identify as dimensions of "immunity to change," have potential to hold a person back from building new knowledge, trying out a new idea, or coming to a new realization. Thus, the acts of challenging and supporting by a hevruta partner serve a crucial role in assisting the person seeking to practice voicing. The partner can ask key questions, offer textual evidence to support a nascent interpretation, and say back what they hear the "voicer" to be saying. In this way, "voicers" can hear their own thoughts with a little distance; can hear themselves be heard; can amend, add, and alter the original interpretation.

With the support of a hevruta partner, voicing can migrate to the *interpersonal* space—between the learning partners and the text. When the act of voicing moves to this external space, it becomes an act of authoring as well—to know what you know and say what you think (Gilligan, 2003; Linklater, 1976). External voicing is a profoundly personal experience, connecting individuals to themselves. "To free the voice is to free the person, and each person is indivisibly mind and body" (Linklater, 1976, p. 2). Articulating an idea or an interpretation that has not yet been uttered, that is connected to a belief, emotion, or value that is deeply held by the learner, is akin to what Peter Elbow (1994) calls "resonant voice." He explains resonance as "getting more of ourselves behind the words" (p. 19), precisely what we hope participants can do in text study.

Voicing is a central dimension to this trio of practices. Voicing a nascent idea, a question that is at odds with the prevailing interpretation, a thought that offers a counterstory to dominant cultural assumptions, can be a risky undertaking. By understanding it in the context of supporting and challenging, we see that voicing is a fundamentally relational experience. The capacity to reach and articulate voice is nested in mutuality, reciprocity, and trust. For example, Kate [2009], a doctoral student in educational studies, offered, "hearing others voice their feelings helped me to shape words around my own experiences and thoughts."

Voicing also connects the learner to the text. Part of this connection stems from viewing the text as a third partner in the relational triangle. In this way, genuine respect must be accorded to the text. Elie reminded the participants that the text is vulnerable—it cannot defend itself if we are not listening carefully and use the text as a "trampoline" from which to launch our own message rather than that of the text. Such an act would be a violation of the text. Listening to the text and distinguishing its voice from one's own is a refining process, making space for both voices to coexist and dialogue.

If we understand voicing to be an act in which the learner is simultaneously in relationship to self, others, and the text, we can see how complex and demanding a process it is—intellectually, relationally, and emotionally. Voicing requires a strong RLC as well as ample opportunities for practice. As an embodied process, voicing, like any form of exercise, may not come easily at first. To continue to refine and build the ability to say what you know and feel, frequent and regular opportunities for voicing are vital.

Finally, it is essential to recognize voicing as a democratic act. The capacity to locate and say what one thinks, knows, and feels is central in a relational space that values the multiplicity of opinion and perspective. While we seek to create such spaces in our classrooms for children and adults alike, our goal is that the learners will take this ability into the larger world to shape public policy, to voice opposition to inequity, and to harness creativity. Thus, voicing is a key act for social change.

In our seminars, we practiced voicing in a number of ways. In the context of hevruta work, voicing was practiced by asking participants to "say something, even if you are not sure." Elie explained voicing in 2009:

> Voicing is "saying exactly what you think or wonder about without worrying about it." [It] gives those who are typically passive in class a greater opportunity to express themselves; with one consistent partner this becomes increasingly less intimidating than in a whole-class setting . . . To say what is on your mind is not an easy thing.
> (Elie Holzer, video transcript, summer 2009)

Acknowledging the complexity of "saying what is on your mind," we asked the participants to practice voicing by doing the following:

- Allow yourself moments of creative silence.
- Allow yourself to explore your thoughts while talking.
- Push yourself to let your own voice speak on what you believe the story to be about.

- Look to support your interpretation by what's in the text.
- Withdraw your interpretation by pointing to what you have discovered to be its weaker points (e.g., textual evidence that doesn't fit your interpretation well enough).

These voicing moves offered participants concrete ways of connecting their internal and external voices, building on the acts of supporting and challenging that may be offered by their hevruta partner. In this way, voicing completes the trio of interpretive practices. Hadassah [2007], a science teacher at a Jewish day school, reflects on the way that voicing is a necessary part of this set of practices:

> The hevruta experience for me was tremendous in that I felt something throughout the experience. My thinking was challenged. My thinking was affirmed. My thinking was voiced. I was able to approach text which I believed was going to be out of my reach. I was able to develop relationships which I never thought I could have. I was not allowed to sit quietly. I had to take responsibility. I had to be accountable. It was much more than learning how to use Jewish text in a general education classroom to deepen the quality of understanding. In fact, that became secondary in the process of hevruta. I became more aware of the connections between my learning and my teaching. I became more aware of my voice as a learner.

CHALLENGING, SUPPORTING, AND VOICING: CONFRONTING OUR IDENTITIES

The trio of challenging, supporting, and voicing practices was an integral part of the hevruta text study pedagogy offered at our seminars. The impact of these practices, however, was felt beyond the work of interpretation. While we did not intentionally apply them to other dimensions of teaching and learning, the participants shared with us that they felt the reverberations of these practices in their enactments of teaching and learning long after they left the seminars.

One way the participants described the impact was in how they felt themselves confront different aspects of their identities—particularly personal, professional, and cultural identities (Raider-Roth & Holzer, 2009). Such examination of identity set the stage for the possibility of transformative learning. When implementing supporting, challenging, and voicing practices, it is important for teacher educators and professional development facilitators to become alert to the ways in which participants' identities can be evoked. We may not anticipate the self-reflection/examination that can result when using these practices and the internal "work" that may be occurring. The following section offers participants' descriptions of how they reflected on their identities as teachers and learners as a result of this trio of practices. These descriptions highlight the power of these practices. They also serve as illustrations that can help professional development facilitators understand the nature of the internal "work" that may ensue as a result of challenging, supporting, and voicing practices. An in-depth discussion of cultural identities can be found in Chapter 6.

Confronting Identities as Learners

Many participants expressed that being in hevruta partnerships, voicing their ideas, and having them challenged led to an increased awareness of themselves as learners. For some teachers, it had been a long time since they had viewed themselves as learners because all too often, professional development workshops focus on delivery of instruction. Teachers are not often asked to assume the role of learner and confront the meanings and feelings associated with learning these new ideas. For others, their perceptions of themselves as learners were as "deliverers" of the right answer, rather than constructors of new ideas. For example, Deborah [2007], a rabbinical student, commented in this regard:

> I mean obviously I've been in school for so long I must be looking for some approval or something. . . . It just made me aware of that. I mean, I am aware of it. But it made me more aware of it. And it made me realize . . . the advantage of being able to quiet that and to be able . . . to work with the other person, to focus on the text, and not to think so much about . . . "What is the right answer?" And, I mean, this sounds . . . so childish, . . . you said things about yourself as a learner that you're not so happy with . . . and that was definitely [deep inhale] . . .

We hear Deborah becoming aware of aspects of herself as a learner that she was "not so happy with," when she answered questions for approval rather than to further her own learning. We can also hear her trying to quiet the voices that interrupted her learning. She was also able to recognize her strengths:

> I don't paint and I don't really play music. . . . I don't do anything that I really consider artistic, but I guess it did help me appreciate my creativity . . . in terms of the hevruta. . . . The brainstorming, and ideas flying, and . . . being with other people and, being able to . . . voice that and have ideas challenged and, sort of honed and refined and that . . . gave me an appreciation of like the creative process of . . . learning.

Deborah could also see her own creativity through the brainstorming that was part of the interpretive process. The acts of voicing, having "ideas challenged," "honed and refined," contributed her new self-awarness. The interaction with her hevruta partner—using the practices—allowed her to quiet her self-critical voice, and make space for a more creative one. This notion of creativity is central to the kind of learning we had hoped would occur in the seminars. It echoes Duckworth's proposition that "the having of wonderful ideas is . . . the essence of intellectual development" (2006, p. 1). All too often adult learners do not have the opportunity to construct such ideas in professional development settings. The first step in this kind of learning is *seeing* one's self as a learner and *capable* of such creativity.

Another way that the "identity as learner" was evoked for participants during hevruta text study was when they shifted their focus to their partner. While so often learners are concerned with their own learning, and how they are performing (much like the right answer theme Deborah described above), Bev [2010], a high school English teacher, helps us see that the supporting, challenging, and voicing process also shifted her gaze to her partner's learning:

> I mean just as a learner the idea that there's so many things that stick with me from [the seminar]. First off, really listening to what my partner had to say and not just listening . . . to see "what I can say." . . . Really taking myself out of the equation and just listen to him.

Recalling the stance of attentive listening, Bev helps us see her how she sought to attend to her partner in order to learn from him.

Confronting Professional Identities

A second dimension of identity that the participants described reexamining during and after the seminar was that of their professional identities. Many of the participants recounted the ways in which the challenging practices caused them to rethink the kind of teacher, rabbi, or professor they were becoming. For the more veteran teachers, there was a kind of "re-viewing" of themselves as teachers, and taking action to reshape their practice. For example, Tamar [2007], an English teacher at a Jewish day school, explained:

> I was struck by Elie's remark that when we allow voicing without challenging our students, pushing them to clarify their ideas and take their thinking beyond where they currently are, we are simply "babysitting." This prompted some soul-searching on my part, as I suspect that in the past I have been too gentle with some students, reluctant to push too hard for fear of undermining their self-confidence. In class, I was relieved to add some specific challenging

> phrases to my teacher lexicon: "Have you considered . . . ? What do you mean by x in this context? You said x, could you say more about this?"

Tamar's "soul-searching" was liberating in a sense. She was "relieved" to challenge her students more. By recounting the kinds of questions that she could add to her "teacher lexicon" we can see Tamar asking the students to open up their thinking, to expand, to look from another perspective. The role of teacher as challenger was not one who undermined students' self-confidence, but rather one who helped students think more deeply.

Marie [2009], a language arts teacher at a Catholic middle school, echoed Tamar's ideas about the place of challenging in her role as teacher:

> This school year, I have found the word *challenge* continually sneaking into my lesson planning and student instruction. While I have always been a strong proponent of collaborative learning, I have never encouraged active challenges within a small-group setting. The rationale for this came from a belief that good "team players" do not create discontent within their group. By encouraging—even requiring—group consensus, I often times discouraged the challenging of teammates in the false promise of group harmony. I now see it differently. Students are *obligated* to challenge each other, so that in considering the other's point of view, both are strengthened. Because each voicing of an idea involves the risk of challenge from their partner, students are required to provide more powerful evidence for their stance. In this way, "iron sharpens iron"—the partners' valuable ideas are equally strong. As a bonus, less assertive students gain confidence when they take on the role of teacher in the exchange of ideas. Students gain a greater insight into the dynamics of partnership while developing effective questioning techniques. (emphasis in original)

Marie's new way of seeing—moving from what she terms "the false promise of group harmony" to an obligation to challenge—represents a new way of teaching. She has reframed her understandings of the role of challenging in teaching and now expects it from her students, rather than discouraging it. She sees the benefits for all students—the less assertive as well as others who readily speak.

Shira [2009], a rabbinical student and educational intern, considered her role as a teacher by asking herself "to think like a student. How would someone unfamiliar with this text challenge it and challenge me? How should I challenge someone? How, how is this relevant to the world?" In an elegant dance between seeing herself as a student and as a teacher, Shira considers the ways that these practices can be enacted and their relevance "to the world."

We can hear similar threads about the role of "teacher" from Kate [2009], as she reflected on challenging practices in her life as an aspiring scholar and faculty member:

> If I want to ask questions at conferences, or if I want to say, be a dissertation advisor someday, it's not okay to just say, "Yeah, that was great." You've got—even if it was great—you've got to be able to come up with some questions and be able to follow it up and extrapolate to go down different avenues. So anyway, challenging her [hevruta partner], something that I need to work on in all aspects of my scholarship. So maybe that was more difficult than just being asked the questions.

Kate recounts that it is not enough for teachers (in this case, professors and dissertation advisers) to affirm the work of their students. She needs to be able to help her future student "go down different avenues," to consider multiple perspectives and ways of knowing.

SUMMARY

This chapter described the trio of practices of supporting, challenging, and voicing and the participants' responses to learning these practices and bringing them back to their classrooms and homes. When the act of challenging was seen as part of their roles as learning partners, participants were able to take risks in trying it out. The participants also taught us that challenging practices often led to identity explorations, which proved to be fertile ground for learning. While initially destabilizing, the supporting and voicing practices helped steady the participants and helped them consider how they could take next steps in their personal and professional lives.

CHAPTER 5

The Text as Partner

How Content Participates in the Relational Triangle

Text study has been a key component of the learning settings and the professional development work I have had the good fortune to collaborate on and facilitate over the past decade. As a result of these varied experiences, I have learned just how central the place of text can be in transformative professional development, especially in its role as a third partner. I have experienced and observed the text's power to shape the relational dynamics in the learning community. This chapter focuses on the role that text study can play in shaping a relational learning community (RLC), as well as the kinds of considerations that facilitators of RLCs might keep in mind in choosing, studying, and reflecting on texts. In particular, I begin by discussing what I mean by *text*, and the rationale for the different forms that texts took in our seminars. We will examine the ways that culturally situated texts are critical third partners in the teaching and learning of diverse cultures. By engaging in one set of culturally specific types of texts, teachers can consider the ways that texts can be used in the teaching of diverse cultures. I then turn my attention to the sense of confidence that teachers who participated in our seminars described as a result of engaging with these kinds of texts. I argue that this confidence reflects a relational connection with self and subject matter (I and It).

EXPANDING THE DEFINITION OF TEXT

All too often the teaching of history and culture in North American schools focuses on a limited conception of text, which may include textbooks, perhaps a couple of primary source documents, and here and there a video documentary. What is often assessed in standardized tests is mastery of textbook material. Expanding the conception of texts facilitates a much broader and deeper view of culture—culture as a multidimensional human experience, as a living expression of values, beliefs, and traditions (Gay, 2000). In addition, broadening the conception of text to include sources that can be experienced firsthand invites the learner to connect with the culture from a multisensory perspective. Such texts include artwork (visual, performance, music, etc.), archival documents (including personal and business correspondence, newspapers and magazines, etc.), film (actual footage derived from a specific cultural/historical context as well as biopics and documentaries), and physical spaces (such as cemeteries, houses of worship, community centers, former and current neighborhoods in which a given community resided). In this way, the texts can become living third partners in the learning process.

One pedagogical goal of our seminars was to offer the participants the opportunity to expand their definitions of *text*. By situating the seminar learning in the context of the relational triangle, we wanted to make visible the kinds of texts or "It" that can support the construction of knowledge around culture. Sonia [2009], a principal of a Jewish religious school, explained:

> What was most useful to my learning was expanding the definition of text to include portraits, letters, architecture, film, etc. Additionally working with primary sources in an interactive manner, looking for what is not there, and searching for sources to flesh out the story were very helpful.

Sonia's comments are especially instructive in highlighting the connection between the texts themselves and the method by which we worked with the text, echoing the findings from Grossman and colleagues (2001), who argue that content and pedagogy are intrinsically connected. Sonia explained this connection:

> Rather than giving us the information, you provided the sources and the techniques to discover the information. You expanded my definition of a "history text." By experiencing the excitement of the hunt for information, I do not know that I can ever teach the way I did before this class. . . . Using portraits, letters, architecture, music, literature, cinema, etc., teased out an understanding of history that was multidimensional. These texts also encouraged inquiry and exploration to fill out the picture.

Her last comment—that the texts themselves "encouraged inquiry and exploration"—is a central point, reflecting the issues to consider when selecting texts for professional development study. As we will discuss later in the chapter, choosing multiple genres of texts that can resonate and build on one another offered the participants the opportunity to come into relationship with the texts, build deeper understandings, and develop a sense of confidence and agency around the use of these kinds of texts in their own teaching about culture.

Talmudic Texts

The study of Talmudic passages in the hevruta text study was carefully considered. First, we wanted the participants to have an immersive cultural experience. Rather than learning *about* the Talmud and its role in the ways that Jewish culture has come to embrace the studying of its own historical, cultural, and religious texts, we wanted participants to study Talmudic passages themselves. Corinne [2009], a teacher at an elementary urban public school, reflects on this intention:

> I really appreciated the Talmudic texts because (1) they are the embodiment of what Beit Midrash [Jewish house of study] was/is about; (2) [they] helped me add color, texture, and depth to my understanding of Jewish culture as a whole and how it applied to my schemata.

Resonant with Sonia's comments above is her suggestion that the texts encourage inquiry; Talmudic texts can do just this. Paul [2009], a high school English teacher, commented that "the ambiguity of the Talmudic readings was quite engaging." Indeed, we selected short passages of Talmudic legends (*midrash aggadah*), which are short narratives that do not require prior knowledge of or experience in Talmudic legal frameworks (Holzer with Kent, 2013). As a genre, they "seem to offer a straightforward meaning [but] students soon discover after repeated readings that the text is more complex than they had thought and lends itself to more than one interpretation" (Holzer with Kent, 2013, p. 208). These texts easily become third partners due to the evocative nature of the texts.

In addition, by selecting Talmudic passages regarding the teaching-learning relationship, we chose ideas that had more universal themes, inviting multiple access points to the texts. That is, participants did not have to have experience studying Talmud or be Jewish to be able to identify with questions of teaching and learning. Cathy [2010], an urban high school English teacher, explained how the Talmudic texts and the hevruta practices served as a bridge to other domains of her life, including "interpersonal relationships and secular classroom learning":

> The Talmud texts were very rich in their simplicity and complexity. We could delve into the text and its issues by focusing on just a few key lines. Although studying Talmud is one of the most serious and lengthy types of Jewish learning, we were able to use these texts to practice questioning, listening, challenging and supporting, interpreting, and making connections in a very general sense that could readily be applied to interpersonal relationships and secular classroom learning.

The last sentence of Cathy's narrative underscores the importance of the methodology of hevruta text study, the methodology by which we studied these passages (see Chapter 3). This relational pedagogy facilitated a connection between the content and process of studying the Talmudic passages with innovative ideas for how Cathy might apply her learning in her own relationships and classroom.

Cathy's comments also accentuate core rationales for focusing on Talmudic texts. The history of Talmudic study has been one of questioning and examining multiple interpretations in order to derive as deep an understanding as possible. The very layout of a Talmud page, with the focal text in the center surrounded by multiple interpretations by different rabbinic commentators, suggests that no one interpretation is correct.[1] Studying Talmudic texts helped convey the fundamental concept that key to understanding Jewish texts (even sacred and seemingly authoritative texts) is to engage them intentionally and question them, without losing sight of their potential for imparting wisdom across time and space.

Place as Text

A central aspect of the seminars was a field trip to key sites in Cincinnati reflecting the history of the Jewish community in the city. Seen as a microcosm of the American Jewish experience, the city's history reflects trends and themes common to the history of American Jewry, such as immigration, economic challenges, social ostracism and acceptance, civic contributions, and communal solidarity. Each field trip included visits to the "Old Jewish Burial Ground" (the oldest American Jewish cemetery west of the Alleghenies); another cemetery still in use where former religious and communal leaders of the community are buried; the Plum Street Temple (a National Historic Landmark built by the renowned rabbi Isaac Mayer Wise); the Phoenix Club (formerly a German Jewish gentleman's club, built at a time when Jews were excluded from the Cincinnati Club), the current Jewish community center; and the old Adath Israel Congregation building, which is today home to the Southern Baptist Church. During the trip we asked participants to consider the places as texts and used the historiographic inquiry process to examine the spaces (see Chapter 3). This approach was novel for many participants, as reflected in Bev's [2010] comment: "Never have I really looked at buildings or structures to analyze them. Never." Similarly, Paul [2009] recounted the novelty of this approach:

> Furthermore, the idea of a physical place as a canvas on which the stories of individuals, a community, even an entire society could be painted was a revelation for me. Our field trip on the second-to-the-last day was enlightening, to say the least, and, frankly, all too brief. As a concrete learner, I appreciated the opportunity to engage in a

tangible experience that helped the historical information presented earlier in the week continue to gel in my mind.

Expanding the concept of text to include physical places that could be seen as canvases on which people paint their stories is precisely the goal we set forth in this seminar. We hoped that the field trips would bring these spaces alive as texts with a voice, and that experiencing them firsthand would help the participants learn to listen to these voices. In other words, we hoped that these trips would help build a stronger I-It (learner-subject matter) relationship.

Interestingly, the trips also offered participants the opportunity to build relationships with the larger issues of American Jewish society and culture. In addition to attesting to the strengthening of the relationship between the learner and the text, participants told us that they connected more strongly to the fabric of American Jewish history and culture.

Sonia [2009] eloquently explained:

> Visiting the historic site/texts gave a picture of the Jewish immigration/migration to/in Cincinnati. The cemetery and the buildings were not just the markers of the history of the Jews of Cincinnati, but represented the hopes, dreams, aspirations, and successes of the community and the people who lived that history. They allowed me to see that history in the context of the society around it.

Listening to Sonia in this way—being able to "see that history in the context of society"—we can hear a connection to the circle that surrounds the relational triangle, the dynamics and forces of culture (see Figure 5.1).

Figure 5.1. The Self-Text-Context Dynamics in the Relational Triangle

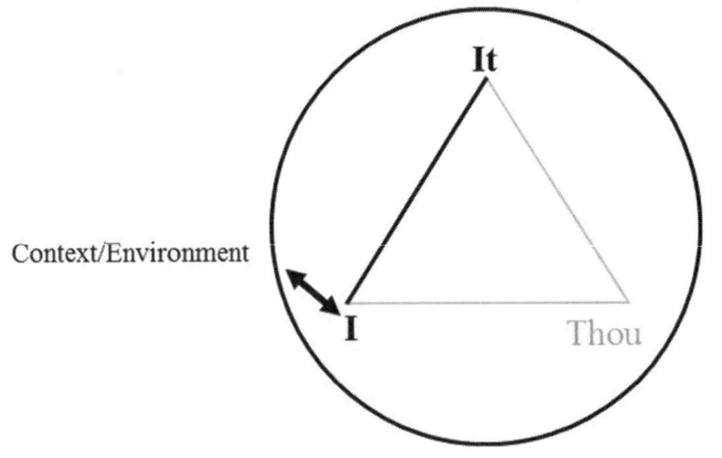

Film as Text

Film was another form of text that we used in all the seminars, both as primary source historical documents and as secondary educational sources. Our aim was to model the possibility for using film in humanities courses as well as to create a learning experience for the participants in and of itself. The primary sources were ones that could evoke a pivotal historical moment. For example, we screened the moving speech by Joachim Prinz at the 1963 March on Washington, where Dr. Martin Luther King Jr. delivered his famous "I Have a Dream" speech. While King's speech is indelibly marked in our cultural awareness, Prinz's speech is not well-known. However, it highlights the ways in which the American Jewish community connected to the civil rights movement.

I speak to you as an American Jew. As Americans we share the profound concern of millions of people about the shame and disgrace of inequality and injustice which make a mockery of the great American idea. As Jews we bring to this great demonstration, in which thousands of us proudly participate, a two-fold experience—one of the spirit and one of our history. In the realm of the spirit, our fathers taught us thousands of years ago that when God created man, he created him as everybody's neighbor. Neighbor is not a geographic term. It is a moral concept. It means our collective responsibility for the preservation of man's dignity and integrity. From our Jewish historic experience of three and a half thousand years we say: Our ancient history began with slavery and the yearning for freedom. During the Middle Ages my people lived for a thousand years in the ghettos of Europe. Our modern history begins with a proclamation of emancipation. It is for these reasons that it is not merely sympathy and compassion for the black people of America that motivates us. It is above all and beyond all such sympathies and emotions a sense of complete identification and solidarity born of our own painful historic experience. When I was the rabbi of the Jewish community in Berlin under the Hitler regime, I learned many things. The most important thing that I learned under those tragic circumstances was that bigotry and hatred are not the most urgent problem. The most urgent, the most disgraceful, the most shameful and the most tragic problem is silence. A great people which had created a great civilization had become a nation of silent onlookers. They remained silent in the face of hate, in the face of brutality and in the face of mass murder. America must not become a nation of onlookers. America must not remain silent. Not merely black America, but all of America. It must speak up and act, from the President down to the humblest of us, and not for the sake of the Negro, not for the sake of the black community but for the sake of the image, the idea and the aspiration of America itself. Our children, yours and mine in every school across the land, each morning pledge allegiance to the flag of the United States and to the republic for which it stands. They, the children, speak fervently and innocently of this land as the land of liberty and justice for all. The time, I believe, has come to work together—for it is not enough to hope together, and it is not enough to pray together, to work together that this children's oath, pronounced every morning from Maine to California, from North to South, may become a glorious, unshakable reality in a morally renewed and united America. (Prinz, 1963/2004, pp. 90–91).

Many participants were stunned to view this speech, never knowing the Jewish connections to this auspicious moment in American history. Jessica [2010], a counselor at a Jewish day school, reflected on her identity as an African American woman in relation to this speech:

> It reminded me that you have these two communities with a similar, if not the same, struggle at the same time, and in my learning—in my education thus far, or up to that point . . . the Jewish side of it was never discussed. And it brought that into my frame of thought. . . . It was just so odd that again . . . it wasn't there for me before.
>
> It was happening at the same time, literally. Like I've taken a million and one AFAS [African American Studies] classes, like that's my second major and all that . . . and March on Washington . . . I did a 5th-grade project about the March on Washington where I interviewed someone who was there. It was—again, nothing that—never brought up. Never brought up.

Jessica's surprise at learning about Prinz's speech reflected a larger sense in the group about the common struggles in the African American and Jewish communities in their search for freedom from oppression. While we were careful to contextualize the complex relationship between these two communities, our goal was to situate the study of American Jewish culture within the larger context of American society and culture by focusing on the critical themes of liberty and human rights as well as slavery and freedom.

Another example of a primary source film was a video clip of Billie Holiday singing the searing song "Strange Fruit," written by the American Jewish-born high school teacher Abel Meeropol:

> Southern trees bear a strange fruit
> Blood on the leaves and blood at the root
> Black bodies swingin' in the Southern breeze
> Strange fruit hangin' from the poplar trees
> Pastoral scene of the gallant South
> The bulgin' eyes and the twisted mouth
> Scent of magnolias sweet and fresh
> Then the sudden smell of burnin' flesh
> Here is a fruit for the crows to pluck

For the rain to gather, for the wind to suck
For the sun to rot, for the tree to drop
Here is a strange and bitter crop (1937, p. 17)

Meeropol wrote this poem and set it to music in the late 1930s in response to his deep distress over a lynching he witnessed in a photo. According to Baker (2002), "Meeropol's ultimate aim in writing 'Strange Fruit' was to protest injustice and to work for the passage of an anti-lynching bill" that was the subject of protracted fight in Congress (p. 54). The song was originally performed at a New York Teachers' Union meeting and later brought to Billie Holiday. The fact that this well-known song was written by a schoolteacher, as an act of activism, helped situate this text as part of "our" legacy as teachers. As with the Prinz speech, we used this text as a way to explore how American Jews intersected with the larger sense of American community at a crucial historical juncture when questions of equality, equity, racism, and freedom were at the forefront of the cultural scene. Such artifacts offered participants the opportunity to experience how the study of one particular culture can give rise to cross-cultural discussions of common concern. These intersections offered participants' multiple entry points of connection, from cultural identity perspectives (e.g., Jewish Americans, African Americans, those committed to antiracist, antibias education), to professional identity perspectives (e.g., teachers, writers, activists, musicians), to personal identity perspectives (e.g., emotional, familial, intellectual experiences). While these identity categories overlap with one another, I separate them here to illustrate the different pathways into connection with this text.

A second form of film we introduced as focal texts of the seminar were contemporary reflections of American Jewish society. A core film text that we used in each of the seminars was *The Tribe* (2005), written and produced by Tiffany Shlain. This 18-minute film offers an engaging overview of the multiplicity of American Jewish identities and affiliations and asks the larger question of what it means to be a member of a tribe. For many participants, the idea of multiple ways of being Jewish and identifying as a Jew was novel and helped them see Jewish culture within the larger American cultural landscape. Corrine [2009] reflected on viewing *The Tribe*:

> [I] learned . . . that various subgroups (Jews, Christians, Masons, Native Americans, Asian Americans, African Americans, etc.), living under the broader cultural context (the United States), share very similar identity problems in that there are often several subgroups within the subgroup. Thus, when some form of cultural medium portrays just one of the many subgroups, those of the main subgroup raise a hue and cry because they do not identify with that particular subgroup of the subgroup.

By highlighting the connections between various cultural groups within the United States, Corrine identified common cultural challenges that minority groups may experience—that of multiplicity of identity and the violation of feeling misrepresented. Jessica [2010] expressed a similar kind of learning:

> I had not previously viewed *The Tribe* or heard Joachim Prinz's speech, but both were responsible for helping me to shape (or maybe I should say reshape) my notions of Jewish identity and the linkage between Jews and American society.

By linking Prinz's speech and *The Tribe*, Jessica helps us see that studying film as text offered important opportunities for the participants to build new understandings of Jewish culture and American society at large. While one film documented a historical event (the Prinz speech) and the other was a documentary of an idea—"What does it mean to be an American Jew today? What does it mean to be a member of any tribe in the 21st century?" (moxieinstitute.org/tribe)—both offered opportunities to "shape or reshape," view or review, the participants' assumptions and understandings about Jewish culture and its place in the American culture.

Art as Text

Similar to our use of film as a primary source was our use of original artwork. To help participants build a sensory and multidisciplinary understanding of American Jewish culture, we studied the Levy-Franks portraits, some of which were painted by Gerardus Duyckinck.[2] These oil paintings of a prominent colonial Jewish family (among the oldest known portraits of a colonial Jewish family) offered participants the opportunity to enter into an interpretive conversation with the artist and the figures in the portraits. What is the emotion expressed? What is the meaning of the figure's open hand? Where is there evidence of a Jewish identity? The paintings portray a sense of confidence, an almost aristocratic sense, with no religious symbolism, no sense of the figure's Jewish origins, and they raised questions among the participants about immigration and assimilation.

To add to the "data" about the Levy-Franks family, we studied one of the 37 letters that Abigail Levy-Franks sent to her son Naphtali, who resided in England. The letter reveals intimate details about her life and worldview. It also illustrates the complex dynamics of life for practicing Jews in colonial New York, an emerging trans-Atlantic hub that was notably Christian in its civic and political orientation. Participants paid close attention to her discussion of intermarriage and the role of Jews as merchants and business owners. Discussions of their Jewish identity are prominent in the letters. The combination of artistic primary sources and belles lettres portrayed a complex set of identities: The portraits conveyed a sense of assimilation and the letters conveyed their Jewish identity more openly. Unearthing this tension of identity and assimilation through the portraits and letters offered participants an opportunity to pose questions and construct possible narratives about the lives lived by the Levy-Franks family members (Holt, 1990). It also offered an important entry point into the study of this period of American history and society and then the opportunity to draw connections with other periods of history where these issues continued to assert themselves for the Jewish community as well as many other ethnic and racial communities.

Theater/Drama as Text

During our last seminar in 2010, we decided to incorporate theater as text in the teaching and learning experience. In trying to establish a conceptual frame for studying the seminal 17th-century Dutch philosopher Baruch de Spinoza, who was also a key thinker in the evolution of secular Jewish culture, we introduced a variety of texts, including a graphic novel and a staged reading of David Ives's (2010) *New Jerusalem: The Interrogation of Baruch de Spinoza.*[3] This staged reading proved to be a pivotal text experience in helping teachers build new understandings of Judaism. For example, Martina [2010], an administrator at a Jewish educational agency, commented:

> By working through such complicated philosophy through the vehicle of theater, the ideas somehow became more accessible. Pedagogically, both the comiclike drawings of the morning session and the play of the evening were good ways to make Spinoza's philosophy—and his mismatch (otherness) within his time and community—come alive.

Martina's comments concerning the accessibility and aliveness of texts highlight the ways that the theatrical medium invited the participants into the big ideas of the seminar, particularly that of "otherness," or the historically outsider status of Jews and other minorities. Gwen [2010], an elementary teacher at a rural school, echoed this same idea in her reflections on the play:

> The play really made our readings on Descartes, Spinoza, and Mendelssohn more significant, as it gave voice, character, and emotion to a group of people, and a place and time that on paper seems very remote.

In studying a historical time so distant from our own, and trying to enter the mindset of this period with historical empathy (Brooks, 2009), the play created an aliveness of a time—full of voice, character, and emotion. The live text helped narrow the distance of that time and place. This experience of closer proximity to the text, the voice and vibrancy of the people, stories, and ideas that both Martina and Gwen convey, is, in a sense, an expression of their own connectedness to the text.

Liliana [2010], a humanities teacher at an independent school, resonated with this sense of closeness to the play as text. She commented, "During the play there were many times I wanted to talk to the characters. I felt very involved and touched by both the dialogue and the performance." This sense of wanting to talk with the characters—a vivid personification of dialogue with the text as a third partner—was particularly heightened during the play reading.

The full-bodied experience of the play that Liliana, Martina, and Gwen describe is akin to the immersive experience of hevruta study of Talmudic texts. Texts that could be remote in terms of time and place are brought alive and into relationship by virtue of the text and the medium by which they are engaged (a staged reading rather than only reading the script; hevruta text study of Talmud rather than didactic instruction of the text). These are important lessons in considering the kinds of texts and pedagogies we choose in developing RLCs focusing on history and culture.

Such proximity to a text can also elicit emotional responses, which offer opportunities for deeper connection as well as possibilities for disconnection. Jim [2010], a high school social studies teacher, commented:

> I talked with my wife about Spinoza on the phone last night on my way home and I couldn't do him justice. How could someone with such deep thoughts be persecuted? It brought out anger and frustration.

The emotion Jim expressed reflects how the play heightened his capacity to connect to Spinoza as a person, as a thinker, and as someone who suffered. The play as text helped bring Spinoza to life as a complex person for whom Jim felt empathy. And yet the closeness that the participants felt to the characters in the play led some to worry about whether the history that they learned via the dramatic text was accurate. Would their connections make it harder to be analytic from a historical perspective? Andrea [2010], a principal of a Jewish religious school, articulately explained this concern:

> I am cognizant of the fact that because my pre-knowledge of Spinoza was so spare, I am in a position that I have to approach with caution—letting the play serve as history. Even though I know the story was dramatized, it was helpful to debrief with Ari, Mark, and the actors. The filling in and correcting of historical happenings and inaccuracies opened up even more understanding for me. The teaching implications for my experience of using drama as text can be huge. The play cannot exist alone as the sole source of info about Spinoza. I know this would never be the case, but I am wondering about films

and other historical fiction taken as history. What's the responsibility of the playwright, filmmaker, writer, etc.?

Andrea's comments underscore the notion that using drama as history raises a question of ethical responsibility on the part of the artist who creates the work; she also suggests that we, as teachers, have distinctive responsibilities with respect to contextualizing dramatized history. As teachers and teacher educators, we must be able to ask questions about the point of view, perspectives, and liberties the artist might have assumed in order to render a creative work. While Andrea offers this key question about drama, it is relevant for all artistic texts that reflect a historical time—literature, visual art, film. Her concern speaks to the centrality of studying multiple texts of a particular culture and time period in order to assist learners in constructing as complex and nuanced an understanding as possible.

In sum, by offering a multimedia, multisensory definition of text, our goal was to offer seminar participants opportunities to experience the texts as alive, as open to engagement, as open to multiple interpretations. In this way, we sought to help the participants locate themselves as capable of listening to, observing, and studying primary texts. It was the building of skills and confidence that we hoped would assist them in bringing such pedagogy and approaches to teaching historical and cultural texts back to their classrooms.

TEXTS AS CULTURAL BRIDGES

In the construction of our seminar curricula, we considered texts to be not only a third partner but also a bridge that could help the participants connect their learning about American Jewish history and culture to larger cultural issues in the United States and beyond.[4] While all the texts offered bridging possibilities, participants often pointed to the literature—short stories and novels—and archival texts as especially useful in this regard.

Literature

In each of the seminars, we asked participants to read at least one piece of literature prior to the seminar. We chose short stories and short novels written by Jewish authors that reflected multiple dimensions and complex themes central to the Jewish experience. For example, Philip Roth's "Eli the Fanatic" (1959) and Franz Kafka's *Metamorphosis* (1915) were selected to raise questions about the idea of Judaism as culture, assimilation, identity, and tolerance. In post-seminar interviews, we were interested to learn that many teachers brought the Roth story—in full or excerpts—back to their classroom. The tale recounts a northeastern town's resistances, biases, anti-Semitism, and insider/outsider dynamics as immigrant observant Jews establish a yeshiva, or religious boarding school. The protagonist, Eli, a secular

Jewish lawyer, finds himself trying to negotiate between the community and the yeshiva, and in the Kafkaesque story that ensues he also finds himself migrating from secularity to traditionalism—a kind of reversal of fortune that raises questions about his place in society and his sanity. Lynn [2010], a curriculum coordinator at an urban charter school, explained the ways in which this story could be a bridge for discussions of diversity and difference:

> I think that it . . . invokes the thought about acceptance, and it doesn't necessarily have to be about being Jewish. You could have applied this to anything—any other community or place where someone may have been different.

As Lynn saw it, "Eli the Fanatic" offered common ground for examining core cultural constructs of acceptance, tolerance, and community. In reflecting on this story, Karen [2010], a middle school language arts teacher, highlighted the insider/outsider dimension of the story: "The Roth piece also spurred my interest into how my students would connect these ideas of insider and outsider in their lives." Cathy also brought "Eli the Fanatic" back to her classroom. The primary theme of assimilation is one that could be "understood across a multitude of cultures" and could elicit deep discussions of "acceptance and tolerance." She remarked:

> You know even in our schools, we have students who are first generation in America, . . . from like Mexico and Panama and Africa, and other parts of the world and so the idea, you know then we can talk about it, well what's different in your life . . . in any of the students' lives, their tastes, their habits, their dress, their speech. What's different . . . in their life compared to their parents' or to their grandparents?
>
> And so the story gave us the way to talk about tradition, cultural traditions and how they've changed and why a community wants to integrate . . . or assimilate. Or in terms of race we talked about passing and so really it was just another angle for some of these larger ideas of identity and multiculturalism and . . . I focus [on] this a lot.

Cathy's narrative helps us see how this text could connect to her students' experiences and identities. She identifies essential issues of identity and multiculturalism—such as integration, assimilation, race, and "passing"—that spoke to her students. The concrete expression of culture—tastes, habits, dress, speech, traditions—provided pathways to these discussions.

Lynn, Karen, and Cathy help us understand how particular selections of literature, ones that are embedded in a particular culture but that address global questions of culture, can become third partners in the study of culture. They can bring alive core issues of diversity and multiculturalism that invite teachers and students to identify with and connect to the challenges that the characters face. In this way, they deepen the study of the culture at hand and offer bridges to larger cultural understandings.

Archival Texts

A cornerstone of each seminar was the use of archival texts. Our seminar drew on a strong partnership with the Jacob Rader Marcus Center of the American Jewish Archives on the Hebrew Union College–Jewish Institute of Religion's Cincinnati campus (AJA), and we were fortunate enough to conduct our meetings and activities in a well-appointed, sunlit classroom as well as to spend time each day in the AJA's elegant reading room. The lovely professional setting contributed significantly to the participants' feeling that their efforts and work were valued and important. While we used the archival documents with different curricular purposes each year, we sought to offer participants the opportunity to engage with letters, pamphlets, and drawings related to the themes of the seminars. We hoped that sorting through artifacts of American Jewish culture would offer another entry point into understanding the lives, communities, politics, and ideas from the seemingly remote past. We were most successful in our use of archival text study in 2010, when we offered participants the opportunity to investigate collections related to sites that they were to visit later in the week on the field trip. They were charged with preparing introductions for their peers to each of the sites based on what they discovered in the collection. Building the connections between these two forms of text proved useful to the participants' learning, as reflected in Martina's comments:

> The field trip was great—made all the more significant because of the work we had done with the archives. It would not have been the same experience to just go on the tour, without our more intimate preparatory work in the archives.

Rinat [2010], a preschool teacher, echoed this connection when she commented that one of the most useful/productive/inspiring aspects of the seminar was "finding a particular gravestone we'd studied in the archive, in [the] Chestnut Street cemetery." Andrea [2010] also highlighted the connections between the archives and the field trip:

> The Archives project, combined with the field trip, enhanced my understanding of Jewish culture in Cincinnati and helped me think about Jewish culture and identity as a whole. As a resident and educator here in the city, I was overcome with ideas and possibilities for my teachers and students. . . . This was my first experience with the glorious boxes and the materials inside. I was thrilled at the Archives's generosity and accessibility. I enjoyed working on the

> project, and during the field trip, each group's gleaning of information during the short time we had to work amazed me. I learned a great deal from each site (text).

The combination of archival documents as texts and place as text provided a springboard for thinking about the wholeness of Jewish culture. This kind of wholeness, or coming together of multiple dimensions, was precisely our goal in using these texts.

As it was for Andrea, this was many teachers' first time working in an archive of any sort and, as such, the experience presented both opportunities and challenges. For some, working with original letters, pamphlets, envelopes, and other documents replete with handwritten marginalia was exciting and invigorating. Martina [2010] reflected:

> It was great to have the chance to work with the archives—I found it to be really engaging work. It was a "teaser," as we only scratched the surface in this arena, but it was good initial training. I would have been interested in more discussion about how to weave together the pieces from the archives into a larger whole—how to acknowledge the gaps versus constructing likely scenarios for filling in the gaps. (For example, I found myself on the tour of Cincinnati wondering what information came from the archives; what was an educated guess; and what was a fabrication, put there for dramatic effect.)

Martina's comments are important in helping us understand the need for even greater contextualization of the participants' archival work. Her remarks resonate with Andrea's earlier statements about the staged reading and how to take an analytic stance of historical interpretations that are based on pieces of archival artifacts. This kind of critical stance—inquiring about the nature of the text: its historical accuracy, its implicit and explicit assumptions, investigating the historical perspective in which an interpretation is based—was one we could see the participants building, as they drew connections between the texts.

For others it was frustrating to encounter such open-ended materials, and they wished for a more scaffolded exploration. As we learned from the 2007 and 2009 seminars, when the archival work was a more open-ended experience, the need for such scaffolding is important. For some participants, a preparatory orientation to the archives was useful, while for others it was not enough and the frustration led to a sense of disconnection. For example, Liz [2010], an elementary school teacher, found the orientation to the archives to be very helpful: "[The] Archive [was] informative, varied, and full of unexpected treasures. I appreciated Mark's preparation for the class; it made the material much more accessible." Yet for Teresa [2010], an independent school language teacher, this preparation was not sufficient:

> The use of the archives was sort of baffling at the beginning. We had no idea what to do, because we had no idea what was expected. At the end, it made sense and it was quite fun. It gave me a new way to look at research.

Others they wished there had been more freedom in the archives. Jim [2010] commented:

> I have had very little experience with using archival records to do research. I really enjoyed this aspect of the seminar and wish we would have had a little more time to do research on topics of personal interest.

Karen [2010], however, wished for more academic time in the archives: "I would have liked more time in the archives to dig in to the available resources in preparation for the field trip."

I highlight the differential experiences of the archives and the archival texts to illustrate the complexity of using archival collections. The complexity stems, I think, from the intrinsically open-ended nature of the collections, the need for both structure and freedom, and the importance of building relevance and context. This underscores the need for careful planning and consistently checking in with participants as they engage in this form of text study. Even with the challenges that archival text study poses, the participants' experiences suggest that studying original materials and artifacts related to the Jewish community's past offers entrée into a rich world of texture and complexity and serves as a generative pathway to larger issues of cultural study.

BUILDING THE I/IT RELATIONSHIP: BUILDING CONFIDENCE

The close study of texts in different forms and media was an integral part in offering our participants the opportunity to deepen their subject matter knowledge of Jewish history and culture. In our use of a variety of texts that built on one another and that our participants brought into conversation with one another, our goal was to support their sense of confidence in understanding these texts and teaching similar texts back in their schools. In other words, we sought to offer participants the opportunity to strengthen their I/It relationship. Sonia [2009] helps us see the ways that text study supported and strengthened this interaction:

> Considering the texts in relation to each other was a check and balance to making assumptions. Using the texts in this way did give them a voice and engaged me in a conversation with them. The most

> important question for me now is, What else do I need to know about this text, and where can I get that information?

The experience of highlighting the texts in relation to one another helped amplify the texts' voices and bring Sonia into "conversation with them." The questions she poses are full of agency: What are the steps she can take to deepen her own understanding and connection with the text? It is precisely this kind of agency, voice, and confidence that we found so remarkable in listening to the participants' reflections on the connections between the texts. Such connections stress the importance of using multiple types of texts, and creating opportunities for the participants to find links between them.

Many participants emphasized the importance of building the connections between the texts as pathways to understanding. Liliana [2010], a humanities high school teacher at an independent school, reflected on the connections between the texts as pathways toward constructing knowledge:

> Living Judaism or cultural aspects of this religion/philosophy/way of life is a new concept for me. Reading texts about this topic, working in groups with various methodologies, and watching the play were valuable instances to get the concept.

Lynn [2010] brought back the connection between the Spinoza texts and the play as a high point in building her own understanding.

> The pinnacle in this area was spending the day arguing about Mendelssohn and Spinoza, and then seeing the reading of the Spinoza play. It was so awesome to see our discussions come to life. I experienced in some way what I have tried to do with my students when I was in the classroom and it renews my interest in providing this opportunity for my staff.

In a sense, experiencing the pedagogies and engaging in multiple texts also provided new energy to bring back these approaches to her staff. Teresa [2010] similarly commented on the connection between text and action:

> The fact that everything we read, discussed, or learned was somehow put into practice and it was not just discussion of theory. I feel that I understood what we were there to learn and can put it into practice.

This kind of agency or confidence—the capacity to put these ideas into practice—is central to teachers' power to help their own students engage with historical/cultural texts. The I/It relationship is embedded, of course, in the larger relational triangle, and as such building such confidence is embedded in relational-cultural pedagogies that we discussed in Chapter 4. By "working in groups with various methodologies," and putting the pedagogies "into practice," our participants help us see the integral connection between the pedagogies and texts.

Tamar [2007], a middle school language arts teacher at a Jewish day school, eloquently sums up how her evolving sense of confidence with Jewish texts is embedded in the relational triangle:

> Before the institute, I would not have felt confident bringing in Judaic texts to study with my students. Using the hevruta approach, however, I felt that I was not really teaching the text, but rather teaching an approach to any text, which the students themselves could apply. By taking the "I-Thou-It" stance and trusting that the text would speak for itself, I was comfortable bringing this opportunity to my students. The results demonstrated to me that this approach allowed my sixth graders to delve deeply into both the Torah text and the novel which they had read.

By highlighting the methodology (hevruta), "I-Thou-It," and the connections between diverse texts (Torah and a novel), Tamar illustrates the ways the texts, pedagogies, and relational theory can facilitate confidence in self and trust in the text. By bringing these three dimensions together, trusting the text and herself, Tamar had confidence in her students as well—she trusted that they would be able to "delve deeply" and learn. This synergy between trusting the text, trusting self, and trusting the "other" (our students, our peer learners, our teachers) is the synergy of connectedness. Such connectedness is the foundation for deep and agentic learning.

SUMMARY

This chapter discusses an expanded notion of texts that can offer teachers multiple points of entry into the learning and teaching of culturally specific and oriented texts. Offering multimedia forms of text as well as full-bodied experiential ones such as field trips to significant cultural-historic sites can support a deep connection to the subject matter. In addition, texts rooted in a specific culture under examination in the moment can serve as a bridge to larger cultural understandings. In short, building connections between the texts can be another pathway to understanding and to an enhanced sense of confidence. Such confidence builds a fertile foundation for a strong and trusting relationship between the self and texts, between the teacher and the subject matter.

"I Feel Liberated"

Confronting Identity and Traversing Cultural Assumptions

Professional development that invites deep learning and transformation is both intellectual work as well as an emotional journey. Part of the emotional "content" of this work is the phenomenon of a "disorienting dilemma" (Mezirow, 2012), "disequilibrium" (Kegan, 1994), "destabilization" (Kegan, 1994), or "felt difficulty" (Dewey, 1910/1933) that can happen when confronting new ideas about teaching and learning. Such uncertain moments can be even more intense when the subject matter of professional development concerns issues of culture. Cultural study, especially when it include histories of oppression, can trigger a revisiting of one's assumptions, surfacing of biases, letting go of previous understandings, and constructing new ideas. This process is an integral part of transformative learning (Mezirow, 2012; Kegan, 1994).

Past research on the summer seminars illuminated many moments of participants' disequilibrium, especially where dimensions of their identities were challenged. Participants described challenges to their personal, professional, and cultural identities. As teacher educators, we understood that we needed to become attuned to these identity challenges so that we could support the participants as they navigated through this rocky terrain. Without this kind of support, the challenge that such destabilization provokes could lead to a sustained disconnection and shutting-down of learning. As a relational learning community (RLC), we also began to attend to the different ways the community could serve as supports during moments of destabilization.

In Chapter 4, we discussed the personal and professional identity explorations that can occur when one is engaging in supporting, challenging, and voicing pedagogies. In this chapter, we will explore the cultural identity challenges that participants described as a result of engaging in the summer seminar RLCs as well as the supports that assisted them in traversing this terrain. Additionally, we will see the potential growth that can happen when disconnections are addressed/repaired and new understandings are constructed.

CONFRONTING CULTURAL IDENTITIES

A clear phenomenon in all the seminars was the investigation of cultural identities that many of the participants reported. Across the three cohorts, participants described the ways that "challenging practices" contributed to this kind of cultural identity exploration. As a faculty, we were surprised by the diversity of cultural issues that the participants described, including gender, class, and religion. Clearly some issues were different for the Jewish and non-Jewish participants, but there is no single generalization that would capture the kinds of identity inquiry in which any "group" engaged. Rather, the investigations were profoundly personal in nature, reflecting not only religious affiliation but also family background and life history. As I discuss three cultural dimensions that were evoked—gender, socioeconomic class, and religion—I am alert to the danger of essentializing any one particular dimension of culture and identity (Sleeter, 2012). Identity is a deeply interwoven construct, and any one dimension of identity is bound up with many others. The notion of intersectionality—"the relationships among multiple dimensions and modalities of social relations and subject formations" (McCall, 2005)—is important to highlight in this discussion. Originating in Black feminist theory, intersectionality helps us understand the complex interrelationships between the facets of an individual's culture and identity (Jordan-Zachery, 2007). I highlight these cultural dimensions in an effort to illustrate the depth with which a study of one dimension of culture—such as religion—can trigger the examination of other cultural identities, such as gender.

The three cultural identities discussed are ones to which we became alert during the data-analysis phases of the research studies. There are many other cultural identities that may well have been challenged—such as sexual orientation, race, and age—but they were not discussed during the interviews or written about in the reflections. They were likely bound up in the experiences of the participants. I am aware that the absence of these issues may well result from the relational dynamics within the group and research setting and went unspoken. In our data analysis, we worked with those themes that were voiced in one way or another. As we continue building our understandings of RLCs, we must inquire further into the different dimensions of cultural identity that can be evoked in this kind of setting, using different modalities of expression (such as artistic representation), and focusing our inquiry to these issues.

In examining these cultural identity explorations, the frameworks of "relational images" and "controlling images" are helpful in understanding the kind of introspective work in which the participants engaged. Relational images are ones that "portray the patterns of [people's] relational experience" (Miller & Stiver, 1997, p. 39) and "connote the ways in which we bring dynamics of old relationships into the prism of current ones"

(Raider-Roth, 2015, p. 38). Judith Jordan (2010) explains that relational images can "determine expectations not only about what will occur in relationships, but about a person's whole sense of herself or himself" (p. 107). In a sense, relational images are beliefs that we have about relationships as a result of our prior relational histories. They can be "unconscious frameworks" (Jordan, 2010) that guide how we think about ourselves, how we behave, and what we expect and assume in relationships. Recently, relational-cultural theorists have drawn the connection between the concepts of relational images and controlling images. The concept of controlling images is theorized by Patricia Hill Collins (2000) as "designed to make racism, sexism, poverty, and other forms of social injustice appear to be natural, normal, and inevitable parts of everyday life" (p. 69). These images often have an insidious oppressive nature in that they can be so embedded in cultural patterns that they become "ordinary." Identity challenges can surface these images and unsettle what seems "normal." Maureen Walker and Jean Baker Miller (2004) help draw the connections between these two kinds of images by explaining

> some of the ways that the culture's controlling images become internalized in the individual's relational images, that is, how the external becomes the internal or how the cultural becomes the psychological. . . . The culture itself becomes an agent of disconnection and distortion, proliferating images that undermine mutuality and authenticity. (p. 144)

In a sense, relational images that are enacted upon in a relationship can stem from controlling images "associated with their cultural histories" (Walker, 2004).

The notions of relational and controlling images are important to the discussion that follows because we discovered that some of the seminar practices evoked and unsettled these images. The participants eloquently refer to these images and explain how they negotiated the challenges to these images that they experienced. In the process of these negotiations, they examined facets of their cultural identities, leading to a new kind of learning—one that included personal and professional insights, emotional and intellectual understandings.

Gender

The first cultural dimension that emerged in our analysis was that of gender, particularly for some of the female participants in the cohorts. Specifically, it was our approach to text study that some women found unsettling. The challenging practices of hevruta text study confronted what Brown and Gilligan (1992) call "the tyranny of nice and kind" (p. 53). For example,

Amy [2007], an elementary school teacher from a Jewish day school, recounted:

> I felt like, "Oh, I'm not being nice here." You know, I was brought up to be the nice girl—everybody would like [whispers:] "All I want is for people to like you, [Amy]"; [back to regular voice:] . . . It is not natural for me to challenge anybody's thinking. Or if I do, I try to kinda go *around* the bush about it, and then they don't get the point. So, I need more practice at that, but, yeah, you know, I got started . . . a little bit.

In Amy's narrative, we can hear both the relational images inculcated in the way she was raised and the cultural pressures to be a "nice girl." The image of a "nice girl"—one whose primary goal is to be liked—exerted pressure on Amy not to challenge another's thinking and not to voice her internal truth.

Challenging practices, as described in Chapter 4, elicited this image for Amy and offered her the opportunity to revisit the "nice girl" image, as well as its consequences—people she speaks with "don't get the point" and therefore she is not understood. While a 1-week seminar cannot dismantle an image constructed through a lifetime of experiences, it offered her some practice to get started.

Amy was not alone in raising the gender identity challenges that she experienced. In reflecting on important dimensions of her learning at the seminar, Bev [2010], an English teacher at a suburban public school, mentioned

> questioning the person's interpretation and knowing it's not personal attacks against them. I just thought that was really good, I don't know how much of that is a female trait but you know there . . . might be times where I would feel like you know or maybe something a friend said was invalid but I wouldn't [want] to hurt their feelings and . . . just him saying it like that. I think it's really just liberating.

By highlighting the notion of "female trait" that held her back from challenging someone else's understanding or perspective, we can hear Bev consider her understandings of female images. This image included not wanting to "hurt their feelings" and held her back from challenging her friend, from speaking something that she knew to be true. For Bev, practicing the act of asking questions of someone's interpretations, and knowing that questioning of this sort was invited rather than viewed as a "personal attack," was liberating.

Shira [2009], a rabbinical student, similarly examined the notion of being female by commenting on her multiple roles as a woman and how she experienced challenging work:

> I'm always looking for ways of self-betterment. It's my own personal challenge to become a better rabbi, a better woman, a better wife, a mother. How do I interact in ways with my son that will encourage him to challenge and not be afraid of conflict? Because I was raised to be afraid of conflict. And how do I help him realize that it's safe to ask questions? But also not to be too pushy.

In this narrative, we can hear Shira's reflection on her gendered roles as a mother, woman, wife, and rabbi as well as her fear of conflict. The resonance with Amy's "nice girl" ethos and Bev's "female trait" is clear. She is searching for ways that she can enact and teach challenging acts, ones that can transpose conflict (something she was raised to fear) into challenge, something that can lead to "self-betterment" (Raider-Roth et al., 2014). She highlights the importance of being able to ask questions safely.

In all three women's narratives, we hear a sense of liberation in the work of challenging—a letting-go of a constraining image of "female traits," to a more empowering stance. We hear Shira and Amy reflect on the ways they were raised—"to be afraid of conflict" and "to be the nice girl." We hear Bev reflect on the female trait of not wanting to hurt others' feelings. They searched for ways to begin letting go of these images in search of ones that invite inquiry and questioning, challenging, and honest discourse. The chance to practice this kind of "role-sanctioned challenging" (see Chapter 4)—the challenging that was part of their role as hevruta partners and members of the RLC—occurred for only a week. As Amy recounted, however, it was a beginning, and was an experience, as Shira described, that she brought home to her inquiry about her many personal and professional roles as a woman.

Class

Interestingly, challenging practices also sparked identity challenges concerning the socioeconomic class of some participants' families of origin. Like gender, socioeconomic class has a universal dimension in that it is a construct that cuts across cultural boundaries. How various cultures address, interpret, and define class within their cultures is distinct and culturally specific (this is obviously true for gender and many dimensions of culture). For example, Kate [2009], a doctoral student, reflected on the discomfort of "speaking up," referencing her "working-class" home culture:

> My dad was a steel worker. I grew up in a very working-class family and it was a pretty quiet way of life. I was talking with a good friend of mine about it. . . . She said, "In my family," she had a somewhat similar background to me; "we grew up reporting, not discussing."

As a doctoral student focusing on cultural discourse patterns, Kate was especially attuned to the ways in which cultural contexts shape how people talk with one another. By highlighting the difference between "reporting" and "discussing," she identified how even discussions can be a form of challenging. This led her to new understandings of how being in the role of hevruta partner helped her "try on" the discourse patterns that she believed she would need to master when she becomes a faculty member.

Lynn [2010], a curriculum coordinator at a charter school, also pointed to her class background that was evoked for her in thinking about the seminar:

> I felt . . . very productive and . . . alive during that week. Because there was so much to say and there was a great exchange of ideas that I haven't experienced—with others, either here at work or—in the past. You know, my parents are workers. They're blue-collar workers. . . . They don't really understand what a 4.0 means. . . . It's just you're going to go get your degree. That's great. . . . They didn't have high expectations outside of "you need to have a job and be able to pay the bills." You know?

The discourse Lynn experienced at the seminar was new and different from what she experienced in her youth, and she locates this difference in her parents' class, as "blue-collar workers." She identifies a gap in expectations between her world and that of her parents. She sees her parents as concerned with jobs and income whereas she is seeking an intellectual stimulation that helps her feel "productive" and "alive." Interestingly, she also identifies a difference between the discourse at the seminar and what she encounters at work. While she does not unpack her work context in the way she reflects on her past, Lynn is clearly thinking deeply about how context shapes and invites different kinds of "talk" and exchange of ideas. In listening to both Kate and Lynn, we can hear how the relational images of their families' working-class identity come up against the academic discourse they encounter and employ at the seminars.

As we reflect on the ways that some participants discussed their gender and class identities, we can see how important it is to be attentive to the identity issues that may be evoked for participants in professional development settings, especially ones focusing on the study of culture. In the traditional model of professional development—"one [day] and done," or didactic lectures that leave little space for relationship-building—there are few avenues to address the issues of cultural identity, yet seminar participants tell us that examining these dimensions can be pivotal moments for learning. Without opportunities to address, reflect on, and articulate these dimensions of identity, opportunities for learning are lost. RLCs can provide a sturdy holding environment for this kind of identity inquiry.

Religion

While Kate and Lynn highlighted the issues of class that the challenging practices elicited, other participants focused on the ways their religious identities were evoked throughout their experiences at the seminars. For some who identified as non-Jewish, Catholic, Protestant, or unaffiliated or did not disclose their religious orientation or identity, they saw their religious cultures clashing with the questioning dimension of Jewish text study and the challenging practices that we asked them to try out. For some who identified as Jewish, the opportunity to study with people from other religious backgrounds offered possibilities to "re-view" dimensions of Jewish culture from a new perspective. The sections that follow unpack these varied experiences.

Confronting identity and building new understandings of religion. One response to hevruta text study and the questioning of Talmudic texts by some who identified as non-Jewish was clearly articulated discomfort. For example, Jessica [2010], a counselor from a Jewish day school, explained:

> I found it harder to . . . challenge some things with the text, or harder to question some things because I think that was a lot of . . . the religious connotations that . . . made it difficult. . . . To clarify that . . . I'm looking at a text that has been part of religion forever. How do I question that? How do I even begin to challenge that because who am I to challenge what Rabbi this did versus Rabbi that? . . . I pick up the Bible—it's harder to question some things because, well, if this is the word of God, then who am I to question it? . . . That's some of my baggage that I brought to those pieces. So being able to work through that and that was tricky at some points, to say the least.

In unpacking the complexity of challenging and questioning a text, Jessica further explained:

> The way I was raised was "Okay, you know what, you can have your reverend, your minister and what they say goes, and you go with that" and that questioning piece wasn't always there. . . . That came with me to the seminar and that came with me when we had to—to do certain text studies or certain discussions.

With remarkable candor, Jessica describes her own religious upbringing and the ways that she was taught to engage with a text, which was a more didactic approach. The questioning pedagogy that she experienced in the seminar—in particular, the challenging practices of hevruta text study—was "tricky" for her, "to say the least." Enacting these relational/cultural pedagogies awakened her religious identity and triggered a state of disequilibrium. Such narratives are significant for me as a teacher educator and facilitator of RLCs because these tender, rocky moments can lead to generative questions, productive uncertainties, and disconnections that can compromise learning. Being attuned to these moments can help RLC facilitators discern the nature of these moments and offer a steadying hand, a space to voice uncertainty, and a pathway toward reconnection.

Jessica was not alone in reflecting on her own religious upbringing and identity and the ways it was evoked during the seminar. Liliana [2010], a high school humanities teacher at an independent school, described her upbringing in Argentina and vividly illustrated the challenge to her own cultural identity that occurred in the seminar:

> I was raised Catholic in a Catholic school for 12 years in Argentina and, most of the time, I was receiving formal education, there were times of the political dictatorship. And a lot of segregation. A lot. And . . . anti-Semitic sentiments. So, for me, I, I was raised in this environment in which I was not in touch with people apart from the Catholic circle. I was not exposed to texts that were different from the, the ones that the nuns gave us, right?
>
> So, it was a sort of indoctrination more or less and that's why I felt that that there was a wall. For example, I knew or met someone who was Jewish, I couldn't feel a connection. I couldn't connect myself with that person because I felt that it was my internal wall. I think that was it; that I was raised in that way and I created that wall. That separated me from others. So I couldn't be connected because instead of finding their common ground, I saw the differences and honestly I didn't understand them because I didn't know them.

In this moving and impressively honest self-reflective narrative, Liliana described a wall that held her back, out of relationship with Jewish students, colleagues, and acquaintances. It was a wall of " indoctrination" of "anti-Semitic" sentiments; the segregation and the lack of exposure to texts other than those "that the nuns gave" contributed to a profound sense of disconnection. When listening very closely to Liliana's thinking and hearing the way she speaks of herself, we can hear the repeated phrases of "I couldn't feel a connection . . . I couldn't connect. . . . I couldn't be connected," suggesting a deep relational disconnection with Jewish people and Jewish culture. The consequences of this rupture led to a lack of understanding and knowledge: "I saw the differences. . . . I didn't understand them. . . . I didn't know them." What is remarkable about Liliana's self-reflection is that she is so open about her understandings of her own cultural identity and the parts of herself that were shut down as a result of how she was raised. Again, we can hear the shadows of relational and controlling images embedded in the "wall" she so articulately describes. She insightfully locates the result of these images—a loss of connection caused by searching for differences rather than finding "common ground."

Liliana's narrative also helps us understand the ways that a study of Jewish culture can give rise to participants' self-inquiry about their own assumptions, questions, biases, or worries of being perceived as anti-Semitic. When studying about Jewish culture, it is not uncommon to confront assumptions about Jews and Jewish culture. I imagine this to be true in the study of any culture with which a person is unfamiliar. Learning the nuance, variation, and diversity within that culture can uncover prior assumptions, biases, and perhaps even latent hostility that can feel shameful. The honesty with which Liliana addresses her assumptions and the controlling images that shaped her understanding is deeply hopeful. In the act of uncovering assumptions, she demonstrates the possibility of building new understandings, connections, and relationships.

Liliana was able to build new knowledge because she was not controlled or stuck by this wall during and after the seminar. During a follow-up interview, she described the ways that she began to chip away at the wall and reshape her own understandings and relationships. She described this process by recounting the aspects of the seminar that "worked" for her: unpacking Kafka's novella *Metamorphosis* (1915), the hevruta partnership, the daily singing, the staged reading of David Ives's play (2010). In addition to the structures and texts, she reflected on the relational notion of the learning community: "the collective learning, the sharing. . . . Everybody was respected as an individual. And that's why I think that the wall vanished." The context in which she began to dismantle the wall was one in which she highlights the "collective" learning and the various pedagogies and practices that invited this collaborative approach, such as singing and hevruta learning. She also underscores the "individual" and the respect that each person received. The collective and the individual were tied together through important cultural texts such as literature and drama. It was the synergy of the whole relational triangle—her peer learners, the content, the context—that provided the space in which she began to dismantle her wall.

Liliana described the wall and its deconstruction:

> Of course, I know when I said the wall it was the memory I had when in my youth. But I think that [at] a certain point I *have* that wall. The wall of segregation, the wall of ignorance, the wall of judgments, the wall of not understanding. So in that sense I think that everything that was done, worked towards that end that for me was "okay there's no more wall" and I'm talking, I know I'm talking about a wall. . . . It was my internal wall. I think that I knock[ed] it down. Yeah definitely, I'm . . . more open to and more receptive, more open to understand people from the Jewish community. I have topics to talk about.

With exquisite honesty she describes the controlling image of this wall: "The wall of segregation, the wall of ignorance, the wall of judgments, the wall of not understanding." Her willingness to claim it, to say that she still has parts of this wall, is surely painful. And yet we can also hear Liliana's dedicated steps to "knock down" this wall, to break apart this image, and to begin forming new connections. In listening to the actions she feels she can take now—"talk," "know," "think"—she is now able to be "more receptive" and "more open to understand."

Liliana seems to find a new capacity for openness and receptivity. Her repeated phrase of "I'm talking" suggests that the wall has lowered enough for her to communicate with Jewish people, about Jewish topics. With such openness, the opportunity for mutual exchange, where she can also share about *her* own experiences with colleagues, friends, and students, is also amplified. With increased content knowledge and ability to communicate, she feels more able to learn. This kind of connectedness to self, others, and content is precisely the kind of relational environment that provides what Sonia [2009] termed a "fertile environment for learning." Liliana's story is so important because it helps us see the ways that controlling images—a possible cultural cause of relational disconnection—can seriously undermine the capacity to know. She helps us see the connection between conceptions of her own religious identity and her learning. Her story also demonstrates the essential link between relational reconnection (repair) and the capacity to build new knowledge.

Liliana was not alone in such reconnections and building of new knowledge. As discussed in Chapter 2, Gwen [2010], a middle school teacher from a rural school, unlearned assumptions about Jewish religion and culture, leading her to describe the seminar as a "liberating experience." Letting go of the idea that Jewish people have monolithic beliefs helped her feel "freed up." Constructing a more nuanced and complex understanding of Jewish culture was also a central point of learning for Bev [2010], one that she described as "eye opening":

> I was not aware of their experience. I [thought] that they were rigid in their religion. And that I needed to respect that and—which I still do. But so none of that's changed, it's just that I don't have this preconceived notion that they believe one way.

Karen [2010], a middle school language arts teacher, also highlighted the notion of Jewish diversity and dynamic change as core to her learning on the field trip.

> Each community, small group, individual defines Judaism differently. Judaism is DYNAMIC, not static. It can (and SHOULD) be an ever changing definition—avoid pigeonholed definitions.

For Liliana, Karen, Bev, and Gwen, building more complex and nuanced understandings of Judaism led to a sense of freedom, of new insight, of liberation. Letting go of preconceived notions, of "one way" that cultures might act or believe, proved to be essential in building larger cultural understanding that extended beyond understandings of Jewish culture. Bev explained in her interview that letting go of the idea that all Jews believed one way

> was all eye opening, but I actually have, feel like it has helped me to understand Muslim culture better. . . . I feel like this gave me the words to understand the idea of being a cultural connection towards religious groups versus being like orthodox about it.

The capacity to understand the nuance and variety of Jewish culture helped her understand other cultures as well, building a bridge toward new knowledge. Bev's comment is important in helping us see that the study of one culture can help us learn larger lessons about other cultures. Sara Lawrence-Lightfoot (1997) teaches that "as one moves closer to the unique characteristics of a person or a place, one discovers the universal. . . . *[In] the particular resides the general*" (p. 14, emphasis in original). I would add to this that as one moves closer to the unique characteristics of a culture, of a people, one can discover universal lessons. Traversing the particular to universal in the study of culture can be both unsettling and eye-opening. This is where the RLC can be essential—helping individuals hold the dissonance they might experience and build connections to new insights.

Re-viewing religion and building new understandings. Constructing new cultural understandings about Judaism was not restricted to those who identified as non-Jewish. Some Jewish members of the seminar described that they found themselves looking at Judaism from a new perspective and recounted examinations of their Jewish identity as well. Studying traditional Jewish texts and core dimensions of Jewish culture with a diverse group of colleagues often triggered a "new look" or new perspective on Jewish culture.

Rinat [2010], an early childhood teacher, recounted that one of the most important aspects of learning was this kind of new perspective:

> It was just the experience of learning "Jewish material" in a class that, at least to me, felt majority non-Jewish or very strong presence of non-Jewish participants and it just makes you think about those [materials] all over again.

When I asked her to explain her process of rethinking, she explained:

> Partnering me for hevruta with Jim was almost—in the beginning, I just—I just—I was—I was just so—well, I'm really speechless, but—but just surprised . . . . Just kind of how would—how do I deal with this man who seems to come from, you know—he's—he tells me, "I'm conservative Christian."

In this narrative, we can hear her search for the words to describe her destabilization, which she characterizes as "speechless" and "surprised." As we have seen theoretically in Chapter 1 as well as in the narratives of other participants, this kind of disequilibrium can give rise to inquiry and new learning. The holding environment of the RLC can provide the space in which to experience the rocky moment, and take steps to new understanding. She expanded on this experience:

> To me it was really great. I mean, theoretically, I've always said diversity gives—enriches the conversation, blah, blah, blah, practically the title of my master's thesis, and here I am. Okay. So, just because I read some books by . . . someone doesn't mean that I've been in that conversation. It was an important lesson to myself. . . . It was—it was humbling and comforting and—and exciting. . . . My self-awareness was sharper because I had to be aware—of his reaction and—or any other time I was in conversation with another person in the group.

She highlights that being in the conversation with Jim was "humbling, comforting, and exciting." She had to sharpen her self-awareness to be cognizant of her own perspectives as well as having heightened awareness of Jim's responses. In a sense, we can hear her describe her own increased relational awareness as a result of working with a partner whose background and experience was very different from her own as well as others in this diverse learning community.

Cathy [2010], an urban high school English teacher, described that she too wondered how non-Jews in the group would view Jewish cultural artifacts. When reflecting on part of the field trip where we visited Cincinnati's "Old Jewish Burial Ground," she recounted,

> So when we were in the cemetery this summer I thought a lot about what people were thinking who had never been in a cemetery like that before and what kind of bridges they would have to create, to try to get into the identity or character the people who were buried there.

Not only was she encountering her own reactions to this cemetery; she was also wondering how it might look and feel to those who had never been in a Jewish cemetery before. She found that thinking in this way encouraged her to "let go of what I thought I knew about something or a familiar interpretation" and open her mind up to a new interpretation. "There were moments like that throughout the week when people would ask questions or make the connection with their own religion or their own ethnicity that would help me see it in a very new way." The sense of seeing things in a new way as a result of the connections that others made to their own religion or ethnicity underscores the importance of the diversity of the group in supporting the participants to construct new knowledge. Additionally, Cathy's reference to "moments like that throughout the week" suggests that the ways in which seminar experiences built on one another created new opportunities for participants to constantly sharpen and refine their personal and intellectual connections.

Andrea [2010], the principal of a Jewish religious school, also commented on the importance of re-viewing Jewish culture as a result of the diversity of the group:

> So having this amazing group of people coming from different places and seeing how, I almost felt like an observer. I mean I was definitely interacting with the text and having my own experience but I loved also seeing how other people were interacting with it. And there were certain times during the seminar with certain texts or certain things that I, I almost cringe, like . . . "How are they going to react to, how are the non-Jews going to react to this and then how are the Jews going to react to this." . . . I mean it was very interesting for me . . . to sort of observe as well as experience it. . . . And so I think that was it was significant for me to be in such a diverse group.

Andrea's sense of observer and participant is helpful in illuminating the two stances she felt she took during the seminar. Her strong curiosity about the ways in which the diversity of the group would shape people's reactions placed her in an inquiry stance, not only about the group, but also about herself.

> I feel like the seminar opened my eyes to some stuff that I already knew but I didn't know that I knew about Jewish culture and it was just so ingrained in me. It was just part of my life that I didn't realize it was something that we could sort of tease out and teach to people.

The observer/participant stance offered her the opportunity to reconnect with parts of herself (discovering what she knew but didn't know she knew), and was an eye-opening experience. Andrea described the newfound knowledge as "I really did have sort of this rejoining of like this old part of me that I didn't realize." She expands on this idea of rejoining:

> Like I didn't abandon it. It's not like I left it. I just, I didn't even realize what it was, it's just who was, who I am . . . and . . . my childhood experiences. . . . As an adult the experiences that I'm having are very, very different but I realized that they belong together.

Andrea had separated her childhood experiences, which she described as living in a secular Jewish home, with her adult experiences, as a principal of a Jewish religious school. Rather than only being allowed have one kind of Jewish identity—"secular Jew" versus "congregational Jew"—the seminar offered Andrea the opportunity to bring these two identities together.

Rinat, Cathy, and Andrea help us see how viewing their own culture through the eyes of those who are not part of the culture offered them the opportunity to re-view, or see afresh, aspects of Jewish culture, their own upbringing, and facets of their identity. The dimensions of the relational triangle are illuminated in Rinat's relationship with Jim (I-Thou), Cathy's revisiting her interpretations to allow for new ones (I-It), and Andrea's investigations of her dual identities (I-I). Engaging in this study of culture within an RLC activated the relational triangle and opened pathways for "opening eyes" and "seeing things in a new way."

SUMMARY: THE CENTRALITY OF DIVERSITY IN RELATIONAL LEARNING COMMUNITIES

In listening to the narratives of the participants—Liliana, Bev, Gwen, Karen, Rinat, Cathy, and Andrea—we hear the importance of the diversity of the members of the RLC. Each of them tells us eloquently, honestly, and with candid openness that the diversity of the group first led to a sense of unsettledness, disequilibrium, or surprise. Their listening stance, however—a stance of listening to how a text, a place, an idea, or an interpretation might be understood by someone different from them—led to new realizations, "eye-opening" moments, "seeing things in a very new way." That the members of the RLC came from distinctly different life histories, cultural backgrounds, and affiliations afforded us the authentic experience of sharing multiple perspectives that is part and parcel of Banks's (2009) transformational model of multicultural education (see the Introduction for a discussion of Banks's model).

The power of such sharing is that it can unsettle assumptions and lead to destabilization and loss of equilibrium. These unsettled moments can set the stage for transformative learning, if there is an environment that can support a person navigating this rocky terrain. So a diverse learning community in and of itself will not guarantee the kind of learning that can change a person. A diverse learning community must be intentionally built so that relational supports are in place for the unpacking of new ideas, the release of old ones, and the discomfort that can accompany this process. Facilitators of these learning communities who develop relational awareness, and implement relational-cultural pedagogies, can purposefully create the holding environment for transformative learning.

As has been illustrated, part of the power of a diverse RLC focusing on the study of culture is the revisiting of cultural identity that can occur. Meeting people who differ from one's assumptions of who they "should be" (such as Bev's and Gwen's realization that Jewish people do not all share the same beliefs) can unsettle assumptions about self (asking oneself, "What do I believe?"). Re-viewing one's own culture through the eyes of those who are outside that culture (such as Andrea's viewing of Jewish culture) can trigger a new look into one's own cultural self. It is the unsettling of self, riskily crossing the "evolutionary bridge" of growth (Kegan, 1994, p. 43) to new discoveries about self, others, content, and the context in which a person is learning, that is the process of transformative learning.

Conclusion

> The best history helps us recognize the mistakes that we've made and the dark corners of the human spirit that we need to guard against. And, yes, a clear-eyed view of history can make us uncomfortable. It'll shake us out for familiar narratives. But it is precisely because of that discomfort that we learn and grow and harness our collective power to make this nation more perfect. (Barack Obama, 2016)

When President Barack Obama spoke at the opening of the National Museum of African American History and Culture, he highlighted the importance of being shaken out of familiar narratives and the discomfort that comes from our seeing history anew. At that auspicious moment, he reminded us that learning and growth are rooted in such discomfort and the "collective power" to create a better society.

The teachers in this volume teach us similar lessons. When teachers learn together in diverse groups—where sharing their perspectives, life histories, and stories can shake one another out of comfortable ways of thinking—they stand on the edge of new learning. Yet we know that discomfort is risky too. Discomfort can make us want to run and escape the unsettled, especially when vulnerable feelings are elicited by challenging learning experiences. Discomfort can cause us to dig into our settled ideas because the fear of that new understanding can unsettle further.

As Bob Kegan (1994) writes and as we have explored in this volume, a "holding environment" can provide the necessary bridge to new learning. It can create a pathway through the rocky landscape of unsettled assumptions and beliefs to new understandings. The concept and structure of relational learning communities (RLCs) is a powerful holding environment for adult learning because of its ability to provide opportunities for support, challenge, and voice. RLCs explicitly acknowledge that connections, disconnections, and repair are inevitable in the learning process because learning is bound up with our humanness. From a relational-cultural perspective, human development means growing more deeply and competently into relationships that sustain and nurture our capacity to thrive. A tough but true dimension of our common humanity is that relational ruptures are inevitable, and our courage is rooted in our capacity to recognize and repair those ruptures. Such repair is the basis for new knowledge, growth, and strengthening of relationships.

The capacity to recognize the dynamics of rupture and repair is the essence of relational awareness. To be alert to undercurrents of relational forces affords us the possibility of attunement—to be alert to the needs, desires, and emotion—of those who are committed to learning with us. All of this deep, complex, and growth-enhancing work is part and parcel of the work of RLCs.

RLCs, however, are not therapy groups (though there may well be therapeutic dimensions of the work). RLCs are learning environments where the shared goal is the construction of new knowledge that can change us and change the way we teach. When we create an RLC to study facets of culture, where histories of oppression can be elicited, the holding environment of the RLC offers an essential foundation for letting go of old assumptions and building new knowledge. It harnesses the "collective power" of the group to pave a walkway of new understandings.

The notion of learning in relationship is not a given in higher education or adult professional development spaces. A most common form of assessment, the exam, which elevates individual mastery over the capacity to collaboratively construct new ideas, is the adult form of "don't look at your neighbor's paper" that we see in elementary and high school. The doctoral capstone, the dissertation, measures a student's capacity to create, conduct, and write a lengthy monograph rather than a student's capacity to create a scholarly community, maintain professional relationships when conflicts arise, and collectively work through the stages of knowledge production. In short, most of our measures of growth for adults are rooted in an outdated notion of development—that to be well-developed adults means being able to work in isolation.

And yet many of us in the adult work world know this conception is insufficient. To be successful in the adult world of work means to be able to participate in collaborative projects, to give and take critique, to balance our own needs with those of the group, to have the capacity to listen to diverging opinions and perceptions in order to construct more nuanced understandings. Learning to work in connection does not preclude or exclude the need for an individual to be able to work independently. Learning to work in connection means that the collaborative spaces are safe spaces to grow from and return to, to reflect on our actions in our work, to check our interpretations of a complex moment, to work out remedies to problems of practice.

Learning to work in connection continues to go against the grain of mainstream educational spaces. It is, in the words of Cochran-Smith and Lytle (2009), a "constructive disruption." And it is a necessary one. Learning in connection offers teachers safe harbor for confronting assumptions and building deeper understandings. RLCs are one framework for this kind of substantive and meaningful work. The RLCs described in this volume help us understand that while sharpening our relational awareness and complex understandings of history and culture is important in and of itself for our own growth and development, as teachers we do this so that we can also create similar spaces for our students. If we can offer our young people the chance to learn *in relationship*, we are offering the possibility of practicing the essential skills of living democratically. Learning *in connection* as adults means that we know what that terrain looks and feels like, and we will be better positioned to create such an environment for our students. Carol Gilligan (2016) teaches us that the essence of democracy is dismantling the binaries that divide us. Such unbuilding requires recognizing those binaries and understanding their historical and cultural roots. If we listen closely to the voices from across the divide, we can hear the moral imperative for connection. And it is when we are in connection with others that we can build new knowledge and take action for a more just society.

Guidelines for Practice

This appendix is meant to assist teacher educators, facilitators, and those who wish to create relational learning communities in their educational environments. Specific suggestions are culled from each chapter to provide guidance. These suggestions are not meant to be instructions, but rather helpful strategies for building learning communities infused with relational awareness.

From Chapter 1—Relationships in Context: Foundations for Teacher Learning

1. *Consider the physical* spaces that are conducive to large-group, small-group, and paired work. Spaces should convey a sense of professionalism and comfort and be conducive to learning.
2. *Confidence-building experiences* (such as icebreakers) are helpful ways to build connections between group members and lay the foundation for learning (see pp. 19–20 for more explanation).
3. *Community singing* can help build a sense of group cohesiveness.
4. *Shared food and meals* nourish participants both physically and emotionally and create inviting spaces for building relationships.
5. *Establishing shared norms for learning* is important to make implicit assumptions explicit.
6. *Regular opportunities for reflection* help create an interactive form of assessment that can inform both the participants and facilitators.
    a. *Individual reflection* helps individual learners keep their "finger on the pulse" of their learning and track their responses and reactions.
    b. *Collaborative reflection* between participants and facilitators creates a feedback loop where participants can privately share their learning processes, challenges, and questions and facilitators can respond both individually and to the needs of the group (see p. 22).
    c. *Collective reflection*—a public reflection on the highlights of a day, or a seminar—can help "hold the whole" and make connections between the different experiences of the professional development experience (see p. 23).
    d. *Group composition* is part of the context. Diversity of the group helps set the stage for the primacy of inclusion of multiple voices, life experiences, and backgrounds. As such, recruitment processes that reach out to different communities of teachers is an essential way to invite diverse participants to seminars and workshops.

From Chapter 2—Relational Awareness: Learning to See Connection and Disconnection and Facilitate Reconnection

1. *It is important to create strategies for keeping communication lines open with participants.*
   a. Daily reflections are useful to invite feedback on how participants are experiencing moments of connection and disconnection in their learning. Questions such as "What supported your learning today?" and "What interrupted/hindered your learning today?" can be useful in eliciting such feedback.
   b. When acting as a facilitator trying to read the mood of a group, reflections in the moment can be useful. My colleague Kathy Simon often asks participants in her workshops to hold up 1–5 fingers to indicate whether directions are clear (5 fingers indicate complete clarity), to indicate how many more minutes participants need to finish a task, to indicate their comfort level trying out a new task (1 being the least comfortable and 5 being the most), and so on.
2. *It is important to be responsive to feedback about disconnections.*
   a. It can be difficult as facilitators to hear "negative" feedback: ways in which participants may have disconnected with the facilitator, or with a text, or with an aspect of the curriculum itself. Yet if we ask for feedback, we need to assume a stance of openness. This may require us to first process the sting from negative feedback. Processing with fellow facilitators can be helpful in understanding the content of the feedback.
   b. After processing the nature of the disconnection, it is important to figure out how to create opportunities for repair. Sometimes this will require a full-group action. Other times it requires a one-to-one action with a participant.
   c. It is similarly important to make visible to the participants how you are creating opportunities for repair. This kind of intentional communication helps participants know that you are taking the feedback seriously and that you regard it as central to the learning process.

From Chapter 3—Relational-Cultural Pedagogies: Hevruta Text Study, Descriptive Process, and Historiographic Inquiry

This chapter is practice-oriented; therefore, many of the guidelines for practice are embedded within it. The following guidelines are meant to be "reminders" of some of the big ideas introduced, but readers are encouraged to return to Chapter 3 for the particulars of these pedagogies.

1. *Hevruta text study:*
   a. It is helpful to begin with a pre-course assignment that assists facilitators in getting to know the learning dispositions of individual learners (with questions such as "What kinds of experiences help

support your learning?" and "What kind of interactions might cause you to shut down or disconnect from your learning?").

b. Texts that focus on the teaching-learning relationship can be helpful in both implementing hevruta practices and in raising essential questions about teaching and learning.

c. Structuring this dyadic form of learning helps participants learn core interpretive practices such as questioning, listening, supporting, challenging, and voicing.

d. Emphasizing the ethical and moral stance of dyadic learning—participants are not only responsible for their own learning; they are also responsible for the learning of their partner.

2. *Descriptive process:*
   a. Disciplined observation of a text can help participants see more broadly and deeply and is an integral part of descriptive process.
   b. Describing a variety of texts—narratives, paintings, films, objects—helps sharpen capacity to see by applying the skills of observation and description to different media.
   c. Learning to distinguish between description and judgment takes practice. Concrete tools such as observation logs where observations are recorded in one column and interpretations/judgments are written in another can be very helpful.
3. *Historiographic inquiry.* "Unpacking" a historical text using five different readings can help people connect with the text in a multisensory way:
   a. The *descriptive reading*, much like descriptive process, seeks to uncover as much richness as possible in the text.
   b. The *associative reading* helps connect self—associations, images, emotions, and so on—to the text.
   c. The *questioning reading* asks the participant to articulate that which is unclear, unsettling, or missing.
   d. The *analysis reading* invites the participant to bring the text to its historical context (era, setting, political environs, global events) and offers possible interpretations and analyses of the text.
   e. The *action reading* offers participants the opportunity to consider their interpretations and how they might put them to pedagogical use.

From Chapter 4—Supporting, Challenging, and Voicing: Why This Trio of Practices?

1. *These practices must be enacted within an intentionally created RLC.*

   The relational learning community (RLC) is a critical context in which to practice supporting, challenging, and voicing. This cannot be overemphasized. If someone were to try out role-sanctioned challenging without having worked to create the RLC, these practices could be experienced as unsafe, and trigger disconnections from learning.

2. *These practices are integrally linked to one another.*

   The trio of these practices creates a unique synergy. In the design of professional development (PD) opportunities regarding culture, role-sanctioned challenging, supporting, and voicing all need to be incorporated in the learning experiences in which teachers engage.

3. *It is important to have regular opportunities for individual, collaborative, and collective reflection.*

   Study of culture often triggers exploration of participants' identities—personal, professional, and cultural. These personal reflections are often not visible to the PD facilitator, and sometimes not even to the individuals. They might be feeling uneasy without knowing why. Thus, it is essential to create regular and responsive forms of reflection during these PD experiences. There is good reason to consider journaling where the *individual* is the audience. At other times facilitators may choose *collaborative* reflection, which is shared one-on-one (written or verbal) with the facilitator(s) and peers. In addition, there is a place for *collective* reflection so others can hear about one another's explorations. Often, this is reassuring, and helps participants to see that "I'm not the only one who feels or thinks ________." This kind of collective reflection can occur in the full group, or in small groups.

4. *Supporting practices require mutuality, reciprocity, and trust.*

   When examining the design of supporting practices in PD work, consider those that invite mutuality, reciprocity, and trust. Hevruta, descriptive process, and historiographic practices all invite these stances in different ways. There are other text-oriented processes that can serve this role as well.

5. *Voicing practices require courage and are emotionally, intellectually, and relationally demanding.*

   Recognition of the demands that voicing places on participants is important for PD facilitators. Participants will need breaks between voicing exercises and may need debriefing to attend to the identity challenges that can occur as well. Both individual and collaborative reflection may be useful in facilitating the processing and communication about the issues that surface during this work. In addition to the practices and processes described in this volume, PD facilitators who want to work on voicing can also turn to the theater world for resources (see Allen, 2013; Linklater, 1976).

6. *Acknowledge identity confrontations.*

   It is important for facilitators to make visible the fact that these kinds of identity confrontations can occur as a result of this practice trio, especially role-sanctioned challenging. It can be reassuring for participants to know that such exploration is part of the learning process. Cooperative and collaborative reflection can be used to help participants and facilitators discuss the kinds of identity issues that are evoked.

From Chapter 5: The Text as Partner: How Content Participates in the Relational Triangle

1. *Selection of texts*

    a. Texts need to be chosen that are sufficiently complex, perhaps puzzling, perhaps ambiguous, so as to pique the curiosity of the text partners.
    b. In addition, when focusing on one culture, it is helpful to choose texts that speak to larger themes of the multicultural experience in North America—such as migration, assimilation, freedom, oppression, justice, and equity. As such, while learning about one culture in particular, larger questions of diversity can be uncovered.
    c. Artistic/fictionalized texts recounting historical events must be contextualized within historically accurate primary sources so that participants have the opportunity to analyze historical accuracy and perspective.
    d. If there is the opportunity to use an archival collection for your seminars, go for it! At the same time, know that this kind of work requires special attention in order to create sufficient structure to support those who have never explored an archival collection. In addition, some participants may also seek freedom to explore beyond the structure provided. If possible, it is helpful to offer optional time to explore the collections, with an archival staff member or seminar facilitator available to support this exploration.

2. *Building connections between the texts*

    Offering learners the opportunities to build connections between the texts is important for constructing deeper understandings. These connections also help learners develop confidence and strengthen their relationships with the texts.

3. *Pedagogies matter*

    As discussed in Chapter 3, the pedagogies with which texts are studied are crucial for unpacking multiple perspectives, for diverse interpretations, and for allowing the texts to have a strong voice.

From Chapter 6: "I Feel Liberated": Confronting Identity and Traversing Cultural Assumptions

1. *Reflecting on relational pedagogies:*

    Engaging in relational pedagogies—especially the ones that invite participants to challenge one another's perspectives, including asking questions of the texts—can be especially evocative of participants' personal, professional, and cultural identities. At these moments it is important to pause and ask participants to reflect on the consonance or dissonance they encounter with these discursive moves. The following reflective questions can be helpful:

- How familiar or strange do these challenging moves feel?
- What comes up for you when you try them out?

Journaling at these moments, perhaps sharing with a partner, can help participants keep their fingers on their own pulses about what is surfacing for them. Sharing these emotions and reflections helps build group understanding, and perhaps validation that others are experiencing something similar.

2. *Confronting one's biases, assumption, or latent antipathies:*

   The study of culture can evoke participants' biases, assumptions, or latent antipathies. This can be a very discomforting experience, leading to feelings of shame and embarrassment. At the same time, new learning can uncover and release old understandings. To support the journey to the construction of new ideas, facilitators can

   - Share that such investigation of assumptions and biases is common in cultural study, which can help minimize the shame that may lead to shutting down or disconnecting.
   - Offer journaling opportunities where participants articulate the ideas that they would like to "release," and the emotions they are experiencing.
   - Offer journaling opportunities where participants can track the new ideas that they are constructing.
   - Offer collaborative reflection opportunities (which can be shared with facilitators/faculty or peers for feedback) where participants can articulate the new ideas they are forming.
   - Offer collective reflection opportunities where the RLC can celebrate the new understandings that people are creating.

3. *Building diverse relational learning communities.*

   The findings in this chapter underscore the importance of inviting, recruiting, and actively seeking diverse participants in forming RLCs focusing on cultural study, yet such diversity is not enough. Building a holding environment that can support the sharing of diverse worldviews and perspectives is essential.

Practitioner Inquiry

Research in Connection

When Mark Raider and I began conceptualizing the summer seminars, I also began thinking about the research we might conduct. As we thought about what we hoped the participants would learn, I started thinking about how we could find out what they actually learned. So the design of the research study went hand-in-hand with the design of the seminars. The essential research question that guided the initial study was, "What is the nature of participants' learning during and after the seminar?" I was deeply interested in participants' own understandings of their learning. Similarly, it was essential that this research improve our practice as teacher educators and faculty members in higher education. As such, we positioned this research as practitioner inquiry (Cochran-Smith & Lytle, 2009).

This practitioner inquiry (PI), focusing on the seminar participants' own understandings of their learning, is rooted in my core belief that how we perceive our learning shapes the ways we enact what we know. That is, the more we can trust what we know—trusting knowledge that we can "discuss, use, and depend on . . . in order to build new ideas" (Raider-Roth, 2005a, pp. 28–29)—the more able we are to grow, innovate, and take risks as teachers. Thus, this PI focuses on these values, and illuminates the ways that the seminar participants understand, articulate, and question their learning.

This PI is inherently relational. Not only was the model of the RLC one that was based on relational theory and pedagogy, but also the methodological approach was rooted in the idea that attending to the relationships between the researchers and participants was key to trustworthy findings. The seeds of the research relationship were planted as we studied together with our participants during the seminars. Positioning ourselves as teachers and learners reduced the power-over dynamics that can occur in higher education environments, and took steps to a "power-with" stance (Miller & Stiver, 1997). Part of the way that we assumed this stance was to consistently ask for feedback and then make changes that reflected the feedback. Additionally, when possible, we studied the texts side-by-side with the participants, feeling firsthand the opportunities and challenges that the texts invited. Taking a relational methodological stance meant that we viewed our relationships with our participants as an asset rather than a deficit, answering in a sense the question "What can be known in the context of human connection?"

Taking a relational stance also meant that we attended to the relationships within our interpretive communities (our research groups in which data analysis was conducted) to be sure that each voice was valued and that the power differentials (e.g., professor and student) were acknowledged and minimized in order to make space for all ideas. This stance also meant taking seriously our relationships with ourselves. That is, when we found ourselves in a destabilized state, we paid attention. What was happening in the data, or in the interpretive community, that led to this disequilibrium? What could we learn in those moments? Additionally, it meant paying attention to the associations we made to the data and the findings.

> Association follows the connections, feelings, thoughts, questions, and images that occur as a person encounters another person, idea, place, song, and so forth. This psychological process is at odds with the dominant paradigm of human science research, which is positivistic, rational, linear, generalizeable, replicable and large scale. Indeed, the current paradigm endorses standardization, cultivating a climate of depersonalization and lack of connection. And yet, the very power of the associative process, and the recognition of this form of thinking, knowing, and feeling, for both the researcher and the participant, is what I believe affords researchers unique access to the heartbeat of the classroom, to the pulse of relationship for teachers and students. In this way, the associative process awakens a relational stance and understanding. (Raider-Roth, 2011a, p. 76)

Thus, the combination of learning together with our participants, carefully attending to those relationships during the research process, paying close attention to the connections and disconnections in the RLC, and taking seriously each researcher's internal connections and associations were the essential components of a relational research process.

This PI is also decidedly political in nature. In describing self-study—a form of PI described below—LaBoskey (2007) positions the notion of "political" squarely on the question of "voice":

> Giving more "voice" to the professionals engaged in the practice of teaching in both higher education and the K–12 schools is one of our political reasons for the self in self-study. Like many feminist and post-colonial scholars, we believe questions regarding knowledge and research, e.g., who gets to produce it and how, necessarily involve issues of power. Our claim is that those who are supposed to have, acquire, and employ the knowledge of teaching are quite capable of identifying, generating, understanding, theorizing, and communicating it. (p. 859).

While I do not believe in the concept of "giving voice" but rather in creating opportunities in which voice can be articulated and heard, LaBoskey's argument makes a strong case that those who are engaged in the act of teaching have a unique and important positionality in knowledge generation about teaching and learning. Similarly, creating space to hear the voice of practitioners is an act that raises the question of power: Who has a right to generate knowledge of teaching and learning? The research studies that form the foundation of this book are situated in the belief that those of us who reside in the classroom have the right and responsibility to inquire into our practice and share what we learn. We are uniquely situated to uncover thorny and complicated problems of practice, thinking, teaching, and learning. As Cochran-Smith and Lytle (2009) argue, "Practitioners are legitimate knowers and knowledge generators, not just the implementers of others' knowledge" (p. 89).

MULTIPLE DIMENSIONS OF PRACTITIONER INQUIRY

It is important to contextualize this work in the larger sphere of PI. Cochran-Smith and Lytle (2009) offer a useful framework to understand "the major genres and variations of practitioner inquiry," which include "action research, teacher research, self study, the scholarship of teaching and learning, and the use of teaching as a context for research" (pp. 39–40). They argue that there are common characteristics among these five genres, including

- practitioner as researcher
- assumptions about the links of knowledge, knowers, and knowing
- professional context as site for study
- community and collaboration
- blurred boundaries between inquiry and practice
- new conceptions of validity and generalizability
- systematicity including data collection and analysis
- publicity, public knowledge, and critique. (p. 39)

These comprehensive criteria teach us that PI places the practitioner—the teacher, the teacher educator, the facilitator, the professor—at the center of the research enterprise. The questions and methodology emerge from problems of practice, their intellectual curiosities, seated in their professional contexts. This is not to say that PI cannot be collaborative and invite participants into the framing of research questions and methodologies. There are excellent models of these kinds of PI studies as well (e.g. Kohan, 2013; Stevens, 2014). These criteria also emphasize the rigor that must be embedded in the research methodology, including presenting the work to the public in order not only to contribute to "public knowledge" but also to invite critique that can strengthen the quality of the work.

While I consider the studies at the foundation of this book to meet these criteria, it is difficult to place them neatly into any one category. For the sake of clarity of the research methodology guiding these studies, however, I highlight the ways that this work crosses the boundaries of teacher research, the scholarship of teaching and learning, and self-study.

Teacher Research

Teacher research is commonly thought of primarily as K–12 and preservice teachers' inquiry into their own practice, often in an intentionally constructed group where the research process is shared (Cochran-Smith & Lytle, 2009). Because a primary professional identity for me is that of "teacher," my first studies focused on practices related to my work as an elementary school teacher (Raider-Roth, 2004, 2005a, 2005b). As I am deeply committed to improving the lives of children in schools, I continue to characterize my work as teacher research. I embrace Eleanor Duckworth's (2006) definition of a teacher:

> Someone who engages learners, who seeks to involve each person wholly—mind, sense of self, sense of humor, range of interests, interactions with other people—in learning. And, having engaged the learners, a teacher finds his questions to be the same as those that a researcher into the nature of human learning wants to ask: What do you think and why? (pp. 185–186)

Indeed, my research over the past 2 decades has focused on learners' understandings of learning and the relational dynamics that can thwart and support building knowledge. Additionally, my first introduction to the notion of teacher was that of teacher/researcher and was rooted in the work of John Dewey (1963), Lucy Sprague Mitchell (1934/1971), Carolyn Pratt (1948/1990), Harriet Cuffaro (1995), and Eleanor Duckworth (2006). In all of these scholars' conceptualizations of the work of teacher/researcher, one idea is core to my understanding: that the inquiry of the teacher, of the person who resides in the same space as the learner and knows the learner well, can lead to a form of knowledge that an outsider to the class is not able to construct.

Scholarship of Teaching and Learning

The scholarship of teaching and learning (often referred to as SoTL) has become recognized as an important form of professional development in improving the quality of teaching and learning in higher education. In 1990, Ernest Boyer (1990) wrote the landmark book *Scholarship Reconsidered: Priorities of the Professoriate*. He offered a broadened definition of scholarly research to include "the scholarship of teaching" (p. 16). This idea and phrase, championed by the Carnegie Foundation for the Advancement of Teaching, is now widely accepted as the "scholarship of teaching and learning," which also emphasizes the importance of studying the process of knowledge construction (Hatch, 2000; Huber, 2004). Lee Shulman (2011), who followed Boyer as the president of the Carnegie Foundation, argued that in order to be called "scholarship"

> an activity had to manifest three essential features: it should be public, subject to peer review and evaluation, and accessible for exchange and use by members of one's disciplinary community. (p. 4)

These three features have been core to the research that is the foundation of this book—each stage has been publicly presented and published in both secular and Jewish education peer-reviewed journals. As such, we can consider this work to fit comfortably in the canon of SoTL.

While the scholarship of teaching and learning originated in the multidisciplinary world of higher education, it also has a firm foothold in the field of education. The Carnegie Foundation created the Carnegie Academy for the Scholarship of Teaching and Learning, which focused on the inquiry of K–12 teachers (Hatch, 2000). In addition, SoTL took root in the discipline of teacher education, where teacher educators began studying their own practice as well (e.g., Gibson, 2012; Gilpin, 2007; West, 2013).

Self-Study

Self-study, a methodology in which teachers study their own practice, can be traced back to influences in the 1980s, when Donald Schön theorized that professionals learned deeply within their practice (Russell, 2007). Gaining prominence in the 1990s, and entering the educational research mainstream by the 2000s, self-study of teacher education practices (S-STEP) became a respected form of educational research (Russell, 2007). Vicki LaBoskey (2007) articulately explains self-study:

> Self-study researchers are concerned with both enhanced understanding of teacher education in general and the immediate improvement of our practice. We are focused on the nexus between public and private, theory and practice, research and pedagogy, self and other. Also relevant to self-study methodology, then, are theories about learning and the nature of teaching. (p. 818)

The studies that form the foundation of this book reflect key dimensions of LaBoskey's definition, particularly my concern with improving my own practice as a teacher educator (and that of the faculty of the summer seminars), building strong bridges between theory and practice, and committing to connect our pedagogy to an active research/inquiry stance. While I was less focused on my "self" than traditional self-studies, as a relational researcher, I remained attentive to the connections, disconnections, and repairs that occurred between me (and the facilitators) and our participants. Continuing to remain alert to these dynamics required an attention to self in both pedagogy and research.

LaBoskey (2007) also offers a useful framework for guiding effective self-study research, especially in the ways that researchers' subjectivity shapes the emerging knowledge. She argues that self-study methodology must be "improvement-aimed" and demonstrate "reframed thinking and transformed practice of the researcher"; it must be "interactive at one or more points during the research process"; it often employs "multiple, primarily qualitative methods"; and it requires that we "formalize our work and make it available to our professional community for deliberation, further testing, and judgment" (pp. 859–860). We can hear certain synergies between these criteria for strong self-studies with that of effective SoTL research, especially the focus on making the work public. The public dimension of self-study distinguishes it from routine or informal inquiry into practice, and more formal, structured research. As noted above, "going public" with our findings was an important feature of every step of our research.

Finally, LaBoskey (2007) argues that self-study is rooted in "core values" of "equity and social justice" and so we "must also be guided in our self-study research by our moral, ethical, and political values and ideals" (p. 819). It is our commitment to our students, to those who entrust their learning experiences to us, that we

> engage in the continuous monitoring of our relations with and influence on them—to check for consistency between our espoused theories, values, and aims and our actual interactions and outcomes. (p. 858)

I resonate particularly with LaBoskey's argument that it is a moral and ethical responsibility for teachers to track our relationships with our students and to continually examine the connections between our beliefs, how we actually connect with our students, and their understandings of their learning. In this way, the research underpinnings of this book share a stance with self-study.

SUMMER SEMINAR RESEARCH PROCESS

In the best case, teacher research, SoTL, and self-studies are conducted within a community of researchers who can offer structure, support, critical feedback, and colleagueship. During the 10 years in which I conducted this research, I was fortunate to create and participate in such interpretive communities.

Interpretive Communities

As I teach in all my research methodology courses, the formation of interpretive communities is vital for the generation of rich and complex findings (Raider-Roth, 2005a; Tappan, 2001; Taylor, Gilligan, & Sullivan, 1995). To carry out relational research, it was essential to develop a relational learning community (RLC) of our own in which we studied the interview narrative texts, used descriptive processes, and enacted supporting/challenging/voicing practices. Over the past decade, the Center for Studies in Jewish Education and Culture has hosted these research groups, thereby creating a generative research apprenticeship space for doctoral students, and producing knowledge that is relevant in the fields of both Jewish and general education. In each of these groups, we analyzed data, supported and challenged one another's interpretations, wrote conference proposals, presented at national and international conferences, and wrote, revised, and revised again articles for publication.

None of the research would have happened without the hard work and talent of the doctoral students involved. For those of us who are researching our own teaching in higher education, it is helpful to have the support of graduate students (or advanced undergraduates) who can collaborate, help with many of the logistical challenges, support the work of data collection and tracking, and participate in the interpretive community's data analysis. It was essential to me that this work, however, not only be in the service of my own growth and development as a teacher, researcher, and faculty member. It needed to be a reciprocal relationship, where the students would develop methodological skills, experience, and crucial CV-building experiences, such as conference presentations and coauthored articles.

Ethical Stance

As we planned the summer seminars, we also planned the structure of the research process. Locating and articulating our ethical research stance was essential for the trustworthiness of the studies (see below). To begin, we submitted a proposal of our study to the Institutional Review Board (IRB), the committee at our university that oversees biomedical and human subjects research, and received approval. Employing practitioner inquiry, we had to make it clear that the study would evolve as the research entered different cycles, and so each year we submitted modifications/amendments to our original protocol to reflect the shifting foci of our studies, revised interview protocols, and revised consent forms.

As practitioner researchers who were developing professional relationships with our participants, we wanted to make sure that no participant felt obligated or coerced to join the study. When participants arrived for the welcome reception of the summer seminar, Vicki Stieha, our doctoral research assistant, and I spoke with each person about the study and offered the consent form. It was important to offer the consent forms at the beginning so that people would understand why Vicki was taking notes, why we were videotaping, that their reflections would be saved for helping us understand how their learning unfolded over time. Some signed right away, and others took time during the seminar to think about their participation. From the 51 participants over the 3 years, 1 participant declined to participate in the study, and all relevant documents were removed from the data collection after the seminar was completed. In addition, it was essential that participants understood that they could withdraw from the study at any time, and indeed a few did and at that point their materials were also removed from the data collection and analysis.

Forms of Data

Ethnographic observations. Vicki held the position of ethnographer for each of the seminars, carefully taking observation notes in every session and videotaping many of them. Her fieldnotes were essential in helping us detect moments of disconnection, as well as moments of connection. While the faculty was immersed in the moment of teaching, Vicki was able to see the big picture of the "room" and alert us when she saw hevruta partners who were struggling or individuals who were at sea. Her fieldnotes were also essential in helping us remember the moment-by-moment events of the seminar as we began to engage in the data analysis phase of the project. In 2010, we were joined by Elizabeth Yeager, who also served in the role of participant/observer, and her fieldnotes were informative as well.

Participant reflections and artifacts. Each day participants completed their daily reflection sheets; we responded and photocopied/scanned the sheets and then returned them. The participants' end-of-seminar reviews were also important data, and they were transferred into large Excel spreadsheets so that we could track both an individual's responses to all the questions as well as all the participants' responses to a particular question.

Some of the participants elected to receive graduate credits for their participation. Part of the requirements for earning credit was to write a final project that reflected some implementation of their learning back in their classrooms. These final projects were also part of the participant-generated data.

Interviews. Three to 6 months after each seminar, we interviewed each participant who was interested in being interviewed and whom we could reach. It was vitally helpful to work with Vicki and Mark Kohan in conducting these interviews. As they were one step removed from the teaching faculty but were familiar to the participants, they offered participants the opportunity to speak candidly with a trusted researcher. We talked at length before the interviews began about our protocol and the relational approach to interviewing that we were employing (see Josselson, 2013; Raider-Roth, 2005a). Transcripts were transcribed by Vicki, other students at UC, and a hired transcription service.

Data Analysis: Phases

In the initial data analysis phase, I was joined by Elie Holzer, fellow faculty member from the seminar, to "unpack the data"—to read the transcripts and reflections, look for thematic strands, listen for silences (ideas that were not said and that we anticipated might have been shared), and develop further research questions that stemmed from the first seminar. Using a hevruta method of data analysis—reading the text carefully and using practices of supporting, challenging, and voicing—we explored the ways that presence was activated in this seminar, and it was the first exploration of the ways that different dimensions of identity were challenged. It was in this study that we renamed the I/Thou/It triangular relationship the "relational triangle" (see Raider-Roth & Holzer, 2009).

The second data analysis phase occurred during a weekly research group with Vicki Stieha and Billy Hensley. Our focus was to understand the nature of disconnections that occurred during the first seminar (2007). To this end, we employed the Listening Guide, a voice-centered, feminist, relational methodology developed by Carol Gilligan and colleagues at the Harvard Project on the Psychology of Women and Development of Girls (Brown & Gilligan, 1992; Gilligan, Spencer, Weinberg, & Bertsch, 2003; Raider-Roth, 2005a, 2011a) to help us listen carefully to the participants' interviews (see Raider-Roth et al., 2012; Stieha & Raider-Roth, 2012). This methodology requires multiple listenings to a narrative in which researchers attend to the ways participants speak about themselves, their relationships, and the prevailing tensions in their narratives. Researchers also attend to the silences—that which is "unsaid"—and consider the forces of culture and relationship that quieted the articulation of these ideas, feelings, and desires (Rogers et al., 1999). Additionally, researchers pay attention to their own responses to the narratives, positioning themselves as both responsive and resisting readers (Gilligan et al., 2003; Fetterly, 1978).

The third data analysis phase occurred after the 2009 seminar, during a weekly research group with Vicki, Mark Kohan, and Carrie Turpin. It was in this group that we coined the term *relational learning community* and began to understand the centrality of a holding environment (see Chapter 1) and role-sanctioned challenge (see Chapter 4) in participants' learning process. These findings were derived using the Listening Guide methodology (see Raider-Roth et al., 2014).

The fourth phase was Vicki Stieha's (2010) dissertation and the resulting publications (Stieha & Raider-Roth, 2011, 2012). Vicki's dissertation followed the participants from the 2007 seminar and interviewed them a second time, a year after the seminar. Through the use of a relational and systems theory approach, her goal was to examine the ways in which context shaped teachers' capacity to enact what they had learned.

In the fifth phase, I studied the learning of the participants during our last seminar (2010). I had been struck during the interviews by the extent to which teachers talked about their new understandings of Jewish culture. Using the Listening Guide, I learned how the study of one culture could provide a bridge to constructing new understandings about cultural diversity (Raider-Roth, 2015).

The sixth and final phase of this project has been writing this book. Writing a manuscript alone that was based on the collective work of many is a humbling task. I hope I have honored the work of all of my research partners. The multiple phases of this research are reflective of the iterative process that is integral to an action research process.

Trustworthiness

The notion of trustworthiness in practitioner inquiry is crucial to creating high-quality studies that are credible. Readers may not agree with the findings per se, but they can see that the researcher has been diligent in making visible all dimensions of the research process, provided adequate evidence to support the findings, and examined the data and findings in an interpretive community. Anderson, Herr, and Nihlen (2007) offer a useful framework for considering trustworthiness in practitioner inquiry that reflects the unique conditions, values, and politics of this form of research. They identify five forms of trustworthiness: democratic, outcome, process, dialogic, and catalytic.

Democratic trustworthiness. This attends to the ways in which the participants' perspectives were accounted for in the research. It requires "planfully access[ing] multiple perspectives and voices" (Anderson et al., p. 148). Many methodological considerations come into play, such as creating a sample of participants in which multiple perspectives can be heard and implementing a set of methods for gathering those different voices. We were attentive to this form of trustworthiness, recruiting all the participants, collecting various forms of their reflections to access their voices at different times, and interviewing as many participants as we could.

An important dimension of democratic trustworthiness is member checking. To the best of our ability, we reached out to the participants before each of the articles was published to gather feedback. Our goal in this process was to check our interpretations with the participants, to see where they felt we got it right or missed the mark. In writing this book, I also sent a draft of the manuscript to the participants, indicating in which chapters their words appeared, and asked again for their feedback. Where there were disagreements, I have tried to offer both my understandings as well as those of the teachers.

Outcome trustworthiness. This refers to the actions that may have been taken as a result of the inquiry. Were there multiple cycles of research in order to uncover and deepen the inquiry and resolve some of the questions that triggered the research in the first place? This is a complicated form of trustworthiness because the inquiry into the nature of learning is not one to be "solved," necessarily, but rather deepened. In a sense, because we had multiple phases of research, and we created actions based on learning in the prior phase, we met the demand of outcome trustworthiness.

Process trustworthiness. This dimension reflects the rigor of the methodological process. It describes the ways in which the researcher makes clear "how the methodology was carried out and how it was developed and adapted over time" (Anderson et al., 2007, p. 150). As described in this appendix and in our related articles, I believe we were fastidious in this regard.

Dialogic trustworthiness. This aspect "requires that researchers be able to demonstrate how they came to the conclusions they are drawing and how they have been and are open to alternative explanations that fit better" (Anderson et al., p. 151). Our interpretive communities were a core process for checking emerging interpretations and challenging one another as we developed our findings. In addition, our regular presentations at national and international conferences, as well as submissions to peer-reviewed journals, meant that our interpretations were viewed and challenged by outsiders.

Catalytic trustworthiness. The final dimension of Anderson et al.'s (2007) model of trustworthiness asks "whether the research process has reoriented and refocused the researchers' and participants' understandings of their local context" (p. 151). Essentially, this addresses the question of transformation—to what extent have my colleagues, the participants, and I changed as a result of this inquiry? Catalytic trustworthiness also attends to the ways that the work may have an impact and inspire change beyond the local context. As a teacher educator, my understandings of the relational needs of a learning community are fundamentally changed and deepened, and in this way catalytic trustworthiness has been met. While I cannot speak for my co-teachers in the seminars, I believe that the data discussed in the pages of this volume—the narratives that the teachers shared with us—suggest that for many, deep and transformative learning occurred. By this I mean that their conceptions of learning, culture, and pedagogy shifted enough that they built new knowledge of self, other, content, and context. For some, change in practice occurred as well. For others, new understandings of themselves emerged. As such, I believe that dimensions of catalytic trustworthiness were achieved.

Transferability

Transferability, or "the extent to which" research findings "can be applied in other contexts and studies" (Dick, 2014, p. 785), is often compared to the term *generalizability*. I have selected transferability because it more closely represents what happens in practitioner research. When I read an excellent practitioner inquiry study, I ask myself, "What can I learn from the findings and how might they be relevant to my context?" I do not ask myself if I can generalize their context to mine, but rather, what ideas, practices, or theoretical concepts might be applicable, useful, or supportive of my own setting. Bob Dick (2014) suggests that particular aspects of the design of action research studies support transferability: "diversity of participants and informants, using literatures to test the boundary of application of findings, access to other people with varied points of view, different forms of triangulation and attention to surprise and disconfirmation" (p. 787). These criteria are concrete and useful to teacher educators as we embark on studies of our own practice. Our studies met these criteria over time—with diverse participant cohorts (most clearly in 2010); substantive reviews of literature for each study/presentation/publication; interpretive communities committed to challenging one another's interpretations; presentations of our findings at conferences that invited critical feedback; data sources that included observation, participant reflections, and interviews; and the consistent reflective research practice where we located our moments of "felt difficulty" (Dewey, 1910/1933). The ultimate test of transferability, however, is whether and how you, the reader, locate findings that are relevant to your contexts, find usefulness in the suggestions for practice—derived from the findings in Appendix A—and evoke questions for yourself and your practice that you find inspiring, useful, and catalytic toward action. If indeed you experience any of these, then these studies will have achieved dimensions of transferability.

SUMMARY: A RELATIONAL-CULTURAL MODEL OF PRACTITIONER INQUIRY

The goal of this appendix is to position the "kind" of research this book represents within the tradition of practitioner inquiry. Spanning the genres of teacher research, the scholarship of teaching and learning, and self-study, this book embraces a political, ethical, scholarly, relational, and practical stance. By describing the research processes, including our ethical stance, interpretive communities, data collection, and data analyses, we offer this chapter as a framework for other teacher educators and practitioners who seek to study their own practice.

This framework, a relational-cultural model of practitioner inquiry, builds on the foundational principles of practitioner inquiry: practitioner as researcher, blurring the lines between research and practice, rigor in research design, data collection and analysis—including recurring cycles in inquiry, and going public with emerging findings. The relational-cultural dimension of this model requires attention to the ways that forces of relationship and culture shape all stages of the research process, including the research question itself. This is not to say that the research question must focus on relationship and culture—our original research questions focused on the question of learning. The inquiry, however, centered on the ways that relationship and culture shaped the participants' learning processes. In other words, it was a crucial stance through which we inquired about their learning and listened to their narratives.

A relational-cultural stance meant that we focused on the construction of trustworthy learning relationships with the participants during the seminars. We positioned ourselves as teachers *and* learners. This kind of fluidity in role was essential to our relational integrity—not only were we anticipating that the participants would take risks and enter rocky territory, we knew that we would also likely enter this unstable terrain. By implementing the relational-cultural pedagogy of hevruta text study, the participants also had the opportunity to experience this sort of fluidity of roles. In this collaborative model, partners constantly shift between the role of I and Thou, teaching and learning one another throughout the exchange of interpretations (Raider-Roth & Holzer, 2009).

The relationships built in the learning setting being studied provide a firm foundation for follow-up study, such as interviews and participant-generated reflections. Relational interviewing, in which explicit attention is paid to the dynamics of relationship that occur before, during, and after the interview, is crucial in relational-cultural studies (Josselson, 2013). We know that what people feel they can and cannot say is, in part, driven by the trustworthiness of the relationship (Raider-Roth, 2005a). It is important to attend to these dynamics so that participants can feel free to say what is on their mind. In our summer seminar studies, we considered the participants' relationships with me and the pressure they might feel to please me, given that I was one of the directors of the seminars. It was, therefore, important that I was not the only interviewer;

other faculty and researchers who were part of the seminar also participated in the interviewing process.

As discussed earlier in this appendix, a relational-cultural stance also means attending closely to the relationships between and among researchers in an interpretive community. Bringing the life histories, values, cultural identities, and intellectual curiosities of the researchers to the table means understanding the different lenses through which we see the narratives we are studying. Making these lenses visible invites multiple interpretations and rendering complex understandings, helping us hear the dynamics of relationship and culture that are present in the data.

A word about data analysis is important here, too. A relational-cultural stance also invites the use of analytic methodologies that can help researchers tune into the issues and dynamics of relationship and culture that may be present in the data. A primary methodology for this kind of attunement is the Listening Guide; however, it is not the only approach to facilitate paying attention to relational and cultural dynamics. While a full review of relational and cultural data analysis approaches exceeds the function of this appendix, common features include paying close attention to the silences, attending to researchers' reactions and the ways those reactions might color what they can and cannot hear, and placing a primary focus on relational and cultural themes.[1]

Finally, relational-cultural practitioner inquiry assumes a "research for change" stance. As discussed in Chapter 1, RLCs are built on democratic educational principles, arguing that learning in connection, in trustworthy relationships, encourages all voices to be heard in the classroom. Inviting and honoring multiple perspectives, including and amplifying diverse life stories and histories, and practicing mutual empathy can help diminish the walls that separate us and keep us out of growth-enhancing relationships. This framework invites research processes and findings that build, nurture, and inspire RLCs. Such communities—where all voices can be heard and multiple interpretations, questions, agreements, and disagreement can be offered—lay the groundwork for new knowledge and practices that can help repair our world.

Selected Texts

Core Texts Used at Summer Seminars

Charbit, D. (2002). Rabbinic literature, 1st–7th century. *A historical atlas of the Jewish people: From the time of the patriarchs to the present* (Rev. ed.). New York, NY: Schocken Books. (1992 edition edited by E. Barnavi)

Hart,S,A.(1847).MiltonvisitingGalileowhenaprisoneroftheInquisition.Wellcome Library, London. Retrieved from artuk.org/discover/artworks/milton-visiting-galileo-when-a-prisoner-of-the-inquisition-125949

Ives, D. (2010). *New Jerusalem: The interrogation of Baruch de Spinoza at Talmud Torah Congregation: Amsterdam, July 27, 1656*. New York, NY: Dramatists Play Service, Inc.

Kafka, F. (1993). *Metamorphosis*. In I. Howe (Ed.), *Classics of modern fiction* (5th ed.). New York, NY: Harcourt Brace Jovanovich. (Original work published 1915)

Meeropol, A. (1937). Strange fruit. *The New York Teacher, 1*(12), 17.

Prinz, J. (1963/2004). America must not remain silent . . . In M. E. Staub (Ed.), *The Jewish 1960s: An American sourcebook*. Waltham, MA: Brandeis University Press.

Roth, P. (1959). Eli the Fanatic. In *Goodbye Columbus: And five short stories*. New York, NY: Vintage.

SchlainT.(Producer,Director,andWriter),&Goldberg,K.(Writer).(2005).*Thetribe*. [Short film]. U.S.A.: The Moxie Institute. Retrieved from www.moxieinstitute.org/tribe

Smith, E. (2009). Bilah Abigail Levy Franks. In *Jewish women: A comprehensive historical encyclopedia*. Jewish Women's Archive. Retrieved from jwa.org/encyclopedia/article/franks-bilhah-abigail-levy.

Smith, E. (1997). Portraits of a community: The image and experience of early American Jews. In R. Brilliant & E. Smith (Eds.), *Facing the new world: Portraits of Jews in colonial and federal America* (pp. 9–21, 28). New York, NY: Prestel Pub.

Archival Documents Used at Summer Seminars

"Slaveholders' Bible, 'Bible view of slavery,' a discourse by Rabbi Morris Jacob Raphall before Congregation Bnai Jeshurun." (1961, January 1). New York.

"Abolitionist's Bible, Michael Heilprin replies to Dr. Raphall." (1861, January 15). The *New York Daily Tribune*. Reprinted in M. U. Schappes (Ed.). (1975). *A documentary history of the Jews in the United States: 1654–1875*. New York, NY: Schocken Books.

These two texts offer two differing American Jewish perspectives on slavery.

"General U.S. Grant's General Orders No. 11." (1862).

"General H.W. Halleck's Revocation of General U.S. Grant's Order Number 11." (1863, January 4).

"Letter from B'nai Brith Missouri Lodge, Protesting General Orders Number 11." (1863, January 5). Reprinted in Zola, G. P., & Dollanger, M. (Eds.). (2014). *American Jewish history: A primary source reader*. Waltham, MA: Brandeis University Press.

These three documents reflect the controversy concerning General Ulysses S. Grant's Order No. 11, in which he categorized Jews "as a class" and ordered their expulsion from the Military Department of Tennessee (Tennessee, Kentucky, parts of Alabama and Mississippi).

"Address of the Newport Congregation to the President of the United States of America." (1790, August 17).

"President George Washington to the Newport Congregation." (1790). Reprinted in G. P. Zola & M. Dollanger (Eds.). (2014). *American Jewish history: A primary source reader* (pp. 41–42). Waltham, MA: Brandeis University Press.

In the address of the Newport Congregation, Moses Seixas, the warden of the congregation, wrote to George Washington during his visit to the city. Seixas penned the phrase "a government which to bigotry gives no sanction, to persecution no assistance," which Washington subsequently adopted in his famous response to the congregation.

Notes

Chapter 1

1. While I take issue with one aspect of Mezirow's goals for transformative learning (fostering "autonomy, self-development and self-governance"), his discussion of the environment necessary for democratic and transformative learning is instructive in this discussion (p. 91).

2. All participants' names are pseudonyms. Quotes have been edited to remove "ums." Repeated words are also edited and indicated by ellipses, unless repetition is important to the meaning of the quote. The year in brackets indicates which summer seminar the participant attended.

3. Thanks to Louisa Cruz Acosta for introducing me to this expression.

4. The AJA, established in 1947 by Jacob Rader Marcus, "exists to preserve the continuity of Jewish life and learning for future generations and aspires to serve scholars, educators, students, and researchers of all backgrounds and beliefs" (americanjewisharchives.org/about/).

5. NDSG, which Perrone created in 1972, is "a diverse network of progressive educators dedicated to advocacy for useful, fair, and democratic ways to document and assess children's learning" (ndsg.org/index.html).

6. Wordles are word clouds that represent the frequency of words in narratives in the size of the text and are arranged artistically to display the results. See www.wordle.net.

Chapter 2

This chapter builds on the findings in Raider-Roth, Stieha, & Hensley, 2012.

1. This 18-minute film offers an overview of the multiplicity of American Jewish identities and affiliations.

2. For a more detailed analysis of Sally's experience of disconnection, see Raider-Roth, Stieha, & Hensley, 2012.

3. Slaveholders' Bible, "Bible View of Slavery," a discourse by Rabbi Morris Jacob Raphall before Congregation Bnai Jeshurun, New York, January 1, 1961; Abolitionist's Bible, Michael Heilprin replies to Dr. Raphall, the *New York Daily Tribune*, January 15, 1861.

4. Sonia is using the term "lay teacher" to describe a teacher without formal training.

5. Essay by David Hawkins (1974/2002). See more discussion of this essay in Chapter 1.

Chapter 3

1. As a word transliterated from Hebrew, *hevruta* has a number of different English spellings. Holzer uses "havruta," but I use "hevruta" to maintain consistency with the spelling used in all CSJEC research publications regarding this practice.

2. This approach was developed at the Mandel Center for Studies in Jewish Education at Brandeis University. See Feiman-Nemser, 2006; Holzer, 2002, 2006, 2013; Holzer & Kent, 2011; Kent, 2010.

3. For a detailed discussion of the implementation of hevruta practices, see Holzer with Kent, 2013.

4. The Talmud is a compilation of Jewish laws and ancient rabbinic writings (30 B.C.E.–500 C.E.), including the *Mishna* and *Gemara*. Quotes are cited by naming the tractate (volume), page number, and front (a) or back (b) side of the page.

5. Texts included Talmud: Tractate Ktubot 62b, Tractate Ta'anit 7a, 9b.

6. Jewish Law.

7. The construct of support and challenge is rooted in the work of Holzer with Kent, 2013; Kent, 2010.

8. Many thanks to Kathy Simon for her thinking about internal and external voicing, which helped me shift my own thinking in this regard.

Chapter 5

1. For a clear, well-illustrated description of a Talmud page, see Charbit, 2002, p. 63. This was the source used at the seminar to help those new to Talmud study understand the physical layout and organization of a Talmud page.

2. For a thorough discussion of these rare historical portraits, see Smith, 2009. To view a reproduction of a portrait of Abigail Levy-Franks, go to jwa.org/media/franks-bilhah-still-image/

3. Many thanks to Ari Roth for introducing us to this play and directing the staged reading. We are also grateful to the Cincinnati Shakespeare Company for enthusiastically participating in this staged reading and postshow discussion.

4. In our 2010 seminar, we extended our focus to include some dimensions of European Jewish culture in order to examine the historical roots of secular Judaism. Findings in this regard are also discussed in Raider-Roth, 2015.

Chapter 6

This chapter is based on the work in Raider-Roth, 2015; Raider-Roth & Holzer, 2009; Raider-Roth et al., 2014.

Appendix B

1. For further exploration of relational-cultural studies and methodologies, see the Wellesley Centers for Women website (wcwonline.org). See also Tracy & Sorsoli, 2004.

References

Abu El-Haj, T. R. (2003). Practicing for equity from the standpoint of the particular: Exploring the work of one urban teacher network. *Teachers College Record, 105*(5), 817–845.

Aldrich, R. (Writer). (1979). *The Frisco Kid.* In M. Neufeld (Producer). United States: Warner Bros. Pictures.

Allen, D. (2013). *Powerful teacher learning: What the theatre arts teach about collaboration.* Lanham, MD: Rowman & Littlefield.

Allen, E. (2016). Catholic Memorial students chant anti-Jewish taunt at game. *Boston Globe.* Retrieved from bostonglobe.com/metro/2016/03/12/catholic-memorial-students-chant-anti-semitic-taunts-newton-basketball-game/SYNt0ozzZm84D-iRoSmMRMM/story.html

Anderson, G. L., Herr, K. G., & Nihlen, A. S. (2007). *Studying your own school: An educator's guide to practitioner action research* (2nd ed.). Thousand Oaks, CA: Corwin.

Antler, J. (1987). *Lucy Sprague Mitchell: The making of a modern woman.* New Haven, CT: Yale University Press.

Apple, M. W. (1996). *Cultural politics and education* (vol. 5). New York, NY: Teachers College Press.

Baker, N. K. (2002). Abel Meeropol (a.k.a. Lewis Allan): Political commentator and social conscience. *American Music, 20*(1), 25–79.

Ball, A. F., & Tyson, C. A. (2011). *Studying diversity in teacher education.* Lanham, MD: Rowman & Littlefield.

Ball, D. L., & Forzani, F. M. (2007). What makes education research "educational"? *Educational Researcher, 36*(9), 529–540.

Banks, A. (2006). Relational therapy for trauma. *Journal of Trauma Practice, 5*(1), 25–47.

Banks, J. (2009). Approaches to multicultural curriculum reform. In J. A. Banks & C. A. McGee Banks (Eds.), *Multicultural education: Issues and perspectives* (7th ed., pp. 242–263). San Francisco, CA: John Wiley & Sons.

Banks, J., Cochran-Smith, M., Moll, L., Richert, A., Zeichner, K., LePage, P., Darling-Hammond, L., Duffy, H., with McDonald, M. (2007). Preparing teachers for a changing world: What teachers should learn and be able to do. In L. Darling-Hammond & J. Bransford (Eds.), *Preparing teachers for a changing world: What teachers should learn and be able to do* (pp. 232–274). San Francisco, CA: Jossey-Bass.

Beijaard, D., Verloop, N., & Vermunt, J. D. (2000). Teachers' perceptions of professional identity: An exploratory study from a personal knowledge perspective. *Teaching and Teacher Education, 16*(7), 749–764.

Boyer, E. (1990). *Scholarship reconsidered: Priorities of the professoriate.* San Francisco, CA: Jossey-Bass & the Carnegie Foundation for the Advancement of Teaching.

Brooks, S. (2009). Historical empathy in the social studies classroom: A review of the literature. *Journal of Social Studies Research, 22*(2), 213–234.

Brown, L. M., & Gilligan, C. (1992). *Meeting at the crossroads: Women's psychology and girls' development.* Cambridge, MA: Harvard University Press.

Butterwick, S. (2002). Your story/my story/our story: Performing interpretation in participatory theatre. *The Alberta Journal of Educational Research, 48*(3), 240–253.

Carini, P. F. (2001). *Starting strong: A different look at children, schools, and standards.* New York, NY: Teachers College Press.

Charbit, D. (2002). Rabbinic literature, 1st–7th century. *A historical atlas of the Jewish people: From the time of the patriarchs to the present* (Rev. ed.). New York, NY: Schocken Books. (1992 edition edited by E. Barnavi)

Chu, J. (2014). *When boys become boys: Development, relationships, and masculinity.* New York, NY: New York University Press.

Cochran-Smith, M. (2004). *Walking the road: Race, diversity, and social justice in education.* New York, NY: Teachers College Press.

Cochran-Smith, M., & Lytle, S. L. (2009). *Inquiry as stance: Practitioner research for the next generation.* New York, NY: Teachers College Press.

Collins, P. H. (2000). *Black feminist thought: Knowledge, consciousness, and the politics of empowerment* (2nd ed.). New York, NY: Routledge.

Comstock, D. L., Hammer, T. R., Strentzsch, J., Cannon, K., Parsons, J., & Salazar, G. I. (2008). Relational-cultural theory: A framework for bridging relational, multicultural, and social justice competencies. *Journal of Counseling & Development, 86*(3), 279–287.

Counts, G. S. (1978). *Dare the school build a new social order?* New York, NY: The John Day Company. (Original work published 1932)

Cuffaro, H. K. (1995). *Experimenting with the world: John Dewey and the early childhood classroom.* New York, NY: Teachers College Press.

Darling-Hammond, L., Wei, R. C., Andree, A., Richardson, N., & Orphanos, S. (2009). *Professional learning in the learning profession.* Washington, DC: National Staff Development Council.

Debold, E., Tolman, D., & Brown, L. M. (1996). Embodying knowledge, knowing desire. In N. Goldberger, J. Tarule, B. Clinchy, & M. Belenky (Eds.), *Knowledge, difference, and power* (pp. 85–125). New York, NY: Basic Books.

Delgado-Gaitan, C., & Trueba, H. (1991). *Crossing cultural borders: Education for immigrant families in America.* Bristol, PA: Falmer Press.

Dewey, J. (1933). *How we think.* Boston, MA: D.C. Heath and Company. (Original work published 1910)

Dewey, J. (1963). *Experience and education.* New York, NY: Collier Books & Macmillan. (Original work published 1938)

Dewey, J. (1966). *Democracy and education.* New York, NY: The Free Press. (Original work published 1916)

Dewey, J. (1998). *The moral self.* In L. A. Hickman & T. M. Alexander (Eds.), *The essential Dewey: Ethics, logic, psychology* (Vol. 2, pp. 341–354). Bloomington, IN: Indiana University Press. (Original work published 1932)

Dick, B. (2014). Transferability. In D. Coghlan & M. Brydon-Miller (Eds.), *Encyclopedia of action research* (pp. 785–788). Thousand Oaks, CA: Sage.

Dorph, G. Z. (2011). Professional development of teaching in Jewish education. In H. Miller, L. D. Grant, & A. Pomson (Eds.), *International handbook of Jewish education.* New York, NY: Springer.

Duckworth, E. (2001). *Tell me more: Listening to learners explain.* New York, NY: Teachers College Press.

Duckworth, E. (2006). *The having of wonderful ideas and other essays on teaching and learning* (3rd ed.). New York, NY: Teachers College Press.

Duffey, T. (2006). Promoting relational competencies in counselor education through creativity and relational-cultural theory. *Journal of Creativity in Mental Health, 2*(1), 47–59.

Elbow, P. (1994). What do we mean when we talk about voice in texts? In K. B. Yancey (Ed.), *Voices on voice: Perspectives, definitions, inquiry* (pp. 1–33). Urbana, IL.: National Council of Teachers of English.

Feiman-Nemser, S. (2006). Beit midrash for teachers: An experiment in teacher preparation. *Journal of Jewish Education*, *72*(3), 161–181.

Fetterly, J. (1978). *The resisting reader: A feminist approach to American fiction.* Bloomington, IN: University of Indiana Press.

Gallwey, W. T. (2008). *The inner game of tennis.* New York, NY: Random House. (Original work published 1974)

Garrison, J. (1996). A Deweyan theory of democratic listening. *Educational Theory, 46*(4), 429–451.

Gay, G. (2000). *Culturally responsive teaching: Theory, research, and practice* (2nd ed.). New York, NY: Teachers College Press.

Gibson, K. M. (2012). Influences on diversity in teacher education: Using literature to promote multiple perspectives and cultural relevance. *International Journal for the Scholarship of Teaching and Learning, 6*(1), Article 13.

Gilligan, C. (1996). Centrality of relationship in human development: A puzzle, some evidence, and a theory. In G. Noam & K. Fisher (Eds.), *Development and vulnerability in close relationships* (pp. 237–261). Mahwah, NJ: Lawrence Erlbaum Associates.

Gilligan, C. (2003). *The birth of pleasure.* New York, NY: Vintage Books.

Gilligan, C. (2011). *Joining the resistance.* Cambridge, UK: Polity Press.

Gilligan, C. (2014). Moral injury and the ethic of care: Reframing the conversation about differences. *Journal of Social Philosophy, 45*(1), 89–106.

Gilligan, C. (2016). Strong democracy and a different voice: What stands in the way? In T. Norris (Ed.), *Strong democracy in crisis* (pp. 55–77). Lanham, MD: Rowman & Littlefield.

Gilligan, C., Spencer, R., Weinberg, M. K., & Bertsch, T. (2003). On the listening guide: A voice centered relational method. In P. M. Camic, J. E. Rhodes, & L. Yardley (Eds.), *Qualitative research in psychology: Expanding perspectives in methodology and design* (pp. 157–172). Washington, DC: American Psychological Association.

Gilpin, L. S. (2007). Unearthing the scholarship of teaching and learning in self and practice. *International Journal for the Scholarship of Teaching and Learning, 1*(2), Article 9.

Gordon, M. (2009). *Roots of empathy: Changing the world child by child.* New York, NY: The Experiment.

Greene, M. (1982). Public education and public space. *Educational Researcher, 11*(6), 4–9.

Grossman, P., Wineburg, S., & Woolworth, S. (2001). Toward a theory of teacher community. *Teachers College Record, 103*(6), 942–1012.

Guskey, T. R. (2002). Professional development and teacher change. *Teachers and Teaching: Theory and Practice*, *8*(3), 381–391.

Hart, S. A. (1847). *Milton visiting Galileo when a prisoner of the Inquisition.* London.

Hatch, T. (2000). *Into the classrooms: Developing the scholarship of teaching and learning.* San Francisco, CA: Jossey-Bass.

Hawkins, D. (2002). I, thou, and it. In D. Hawkins (Ed.), *The informed vision: Essays on learning and human nature* (pp. 48–62). New York, NY: Agathon Press. (Original work published 1974)

Himley, M., & Carini, P. F. (2000). *From another angle: Children's strengths and school standards*. New York, NY: Teachers College Press.

Hollins, E., McIntyre, L. R., DeBose, C., Hollins, K. S., & Towner, A. (2004). Promoting a self-sustaining learning community: Investigating an internal model for teacher development. *International Journal of Qualitative Studies in Education, 17*(2), 237–249.

Holt, T. (1990). *Thinking historically: Narrative, imagination, and understanding*. Princeton, NJ: College Board.

Holzer, E. (2002). Conceptions of the study of Jewish texts in teachers' professional development. *Religious Education, 72*(4), 377–403.

Holzer, E. (2006). What connects "good" teaching, text study and *hevruta* learning? A conceptual argument. *Journal of Jewish Education, 72*(3), 183–204.

Holzer, E. (2016). *Attuned learning: Rabbinic texts on habits of the heart in learning interactions*. Brighton, MA: Academic Studies Press.

Holzer, E., with Kent, O. (2013). *A philosophy of havruta: Understanding and teaching the art of text study in pairs*. Brighton, MA: Academic Studies Press.

Holzer, E., & Kent, O. (2011). Havruta: What do we know and what can we hope to learn from studying in havruta? In H. Miller, L. D. Grant, & A. Pomson (Eds.), *International handbook of Jewish education* (pp. 407–417). Dordrecht, The Netherlands: Springer.

Huber, M. T. (2004). *Balancing acts: The scholarship of teaching and learning in academic careers*. Washington, DC: American Association for Higher Education and Carnegie Foundation for the Advancement of Teaching.

Jordan, J. (2004). Relational awareness: Transforming disconnections. In J. Jordan, L. M. Hartling, & M. Walker (Eds.), *The complexity of connection: Writings from the Stone Center's Jean Baker Miller Training Institute* (pp. 47–63). New York, NY: Guilford Press.

Jordan, J. (2010). *Relational cultural therapy*. Washington, DC: American Psychological Association.

Jordan J., & Walker, M. (2004). Introduction. In J. Jordan, L. M. Hartling, & M. Walker (Eds.), *The complexity of connection: Writings from the Stone Center's Jean Baker Miller Training Institute* (pp. 1–8). New York, NY: Guilford Press.

Jordan, J. V. (1992). Relational resilience. *Work in Progress, No. 57*. Wellesley, MA: Stone Center Working Paper Series.

Jordan, J. V., & Dooley, K. (2000). Relational practice in action: A group manual. *Project Report, No. 6*. Wellesley, MA: Stone Center Working Paper Series.

Jordan-Zachery, J. S. (2007). Am I a Black woman or a woman who is Black? A few thoughts on the meaning of intersectionality. *Politics and Gender, 3*(2), 254–263.

Josselson, R. (2013). *Interviewing for qualitative inquiry: A relational approach*. New York, NY: Guilford Press.

Jurow, A. S. (2009). Cultivating self in the context of transformative professional development. *Journal of Teacher Education, 60*(3), 277–290.

Kegan, R. (1994). *In over our heads: The mental demands of modern life*. Cambridge, MA: Harvard University Press.

Kegan, R., & Lahey. L. L. (2001). *How the way we talk can change the way we work*. San Francisco, CA: Jossey-Bass.

Kegan, R., & Lahey. L. L. (2009). *Immunity to change*. Boston, MA: Harvard Business School.

Kent, O. (2010). A theory of *havruta* learning. *Journal of Jewish Education*, *76*(3), 215–245.

Kent, O. (2013). Supporting and challenging. In E. Holzer with O. Kent, *A philosophy of havruta learning: Understanding and teaching the art of text study in pairs* (pp. 123–145). Boston, MA: Academic Studies Press.

Kohan, M. (2013). *Story as an organizing and inquiry tool for educational partnerships committed to social justice, school, and community change* (Doctoral dissertation). Retrieved from rave.ohiolink.edu/etdc/view?acc_num=ucin1384334539.

Kumashiro, K. K. (2010). Seeing the bigger picture: Troubling movements to end teacher education. *Journal of Teacher Education*, *61*(1–2), 56–65.

LaBoskey, V. K. (2007). The methodology of self-study and its theoretical underpinnings. In J. Loughran, M. L. Hamilton, V. K. LaBoskey, & T. L. Russell (Eds.), *International handbook of self-study of teaching and teacher education practices* (pp. 817–869). Dordrecht, The Netherlands: Springer.

Lawrence-Lightfoot, S. (1997). A view of the whole: Origins and purposes. In S. Lawrence-Lightfoot & J. H. Davis (Eds.), *The art and science of portraiture* (pp. 1–16). San Francisco, CA: Jossey-Bass.

Linklater, K. (1976). *Freeing the natural voice*. New York, NY, and Hollywood, CA: Drama.

Lipset, S. M., & Rabb, E. (1995). *Jews and the new American scene*. Cambridge, MA: Harvard University Press.

Little, J. W. (2006). *Professional community and professional development in the learning-centered school* [Best practices learning paper]. Washington DC: National Education Association.

McCall, L. (2005). The complexity of intersectionality. *Signs 30*(3), 1771–1800.

McDonald, J. P., Mohr, N., Dichter, A., & McDonald, E. C. (2014). *The power of protocols: An educator's guide to better practice* (3rd ed.). New York, NY: Teachers College Press.

Meeropol, A. (1937). Strange fruit. *The New York Teacher*, *1*(12), 17.

Mezirow, J. (2012). Learning to think like an adult: Core concepts of transformation theory. In J. T. P. Cranton (Ed.), *The handbook of transformative learning* (pp. 73–95). San Francisco, CA: Jossey-Bass.

Miller, J. B. (1986). What do we mean by relationships? *Work in Progress, No.* 22. Wellesley, MA: Stone Center Working Paper Series.

Miller, J. B., & Stiver, I. P. (1997). *The healing connection: How women form relationships in therapy and in life*. Boston, MA: Beacon.

Miranda, T. T. (2012). Lessons learned from transformational professional development. *New Directions for Teaching and Learning, 130*, 77–88.

Mitchell, L. S. (1971). *Young geographers*. New York, NY: Bank Street College. (Original work published 1934).

Muir, P. (2007). Action research in the scholarship of L&T. *The RMIT Teaching and Learning Journal, 2*(3). Retrieved from emedia.rmit.edu.au/edjournal/vol2,issue3, 2007-issue_contents?q=node/280.

Murray, T. (2005). Exploring the psychological terrain of the virtual classroom: The nature of relationship and power in online, asynchronous teaching and learning (unpublished doctoral dissertation), State University of New York at Albany.

Obama, B. (2016). Remarks by the president at the dedication of the National Museum of African American History and Culture. Retrieved from whitehouse.

gov/the-press-office/2016/09/24/remarks-president-dedication-national-museum-african-american-history

Pratt, C. (1990). *I learn from children: An adventure in progressive education.* New York, NY: Perennial Library. (Original work published 1948)

Raider, M. (2010). Education and Jewish studies. Unpublished manuscript, distributed at Summer Seminar, Cincinnati, OH.

Raider-Roth, M. (2004). Taking the time to think: A portrait of reflection. *Teaching and Learning: A Journal of Natural Inquiry and Reflective Practice, 18*(3), 79–97.

Raider-Roth, M. (2005a). *Trusting what you know: The high stakes of classroom relationships.* San Francisco, CA: Jossey-Bass.

Raider-Roth, M. (2005b). Trusting what you know: Negotiating the relational context of classroom life. *Teachers College Record, 105*(7), 587–628.

Raider-Roth, M. (2011a). Listening to the heartbeat of the classroom: Bringing the listening guide to school. In P. C. Davis & L. C. Davis (Eds.), *Enacting pleasure: Artists and scholars respond to Carol Gilligan's new map of love* (pp. 75–92). London, UK: Seagull Books.

Raider-Roth, M. (2011b). The place of description in understanding and transforming classroom relationships. *The New Educator, 7*(3), 274–286.

Raider-Roth, M. (2015). Bridges to new knowledge: Culture, religion, and identity in teacher professional development. *International Journal of Jewish Education Research, 8*, 7–36.

Raider-Roth, M., & Holzer, E. (2009). Learning to be present: How *hevruta* learning can activate teachers' relationships to self, other, and text. *Journal of Jewish Education, 75*(3), 216–239.

Raider-Roth, M., Stieha, V., & Hensley, B. (2012). Rupture and repair: Episodes of resistance and resilience in teachers' learning. *Teaching and Teacher Education, 28*(4), 493–502.

Raider-Roth, M., Stieha, V., Kohan, M., & Turpin, C. (2014). The false promise of group harmony: The centrality of challenging practices in teachers' professional development. *Journal of Jewish Education, 80*(1), 53–77.

Randi, J., & Zeichner, K. (2004). New visions of teacher professional development. In M. Smylie & D. Miretszky (Eds.), *Developing the teacher workforce: Yearbook of the National Society for the Study of Education* (pp. 180–227). Chicago, IL: University of Chicago Press.

Reichert, M., & Hawley, R. (2014). *I can learn from you: Boys as relational learners.* Cambridge, MA: Harvard Education Press.

Rodgers, C. (2002). Defining reflection: Another look at John Dewey and reflective thinking. *Teachers College Record, 104*, 842–866.

Rodgers, C. (2011). A case of learning to teach social studies at the Prospect School teacher education program. *The New Educator, 7*(3), 215–239.

Rodgers, C., & Raider-Roth, M. B. (2006). Presence in teaching. *Teachers and teaching: Theory and practice, 12*(3), 265–287.

Rodgers, C. R., & Scott, K. H. (2008). The development of the personal self and professional identity in learning to teach. In M. Cochran-Smith, S. Feiman-Nemser, D. J. McIntyre, & E. K. Demersd (Eds.), *Handbook of research on teacher education* (3rd ed., pp. 732–755). New York, NY, and London, UK: Routledge and the Association of Teacher Educators.

Rogers, A., Casey, M. E., Ekert, J., Holland, J., Nakkula, V., & Sheinberg, N. (1999). An interpretive poetics of languages of unsayable. In R. Josselson & A. Lieblich

(Eds.), *Making meaning of narratives: The narrative study of lives series* (Vol. 6, pp. 77–106). Thousand Oaks, CA: Sage.

Russell, T. (2007). Tracing the development of self-study in teacher education research and practice. In J. Loughran, M. L. Hamilton, V. K. LaBoskey, & T. L. Russell (Eds.), *International handbook of self-study of teaching and teacher education practices* (pp. 1191–1210). Dordrecht, The Netherlands: Springer.

Sachs, J. (2003). *The activist teaching profession*. Buckingham, UK: Open University Press.

Schultz, K. (2003). *Listening: A framework for teaching across differences*. New York, NY: Teachers College Press.

Schwartz, H. L., & Holloway, E. L. (2012). Partners in learning: A grounded theory study of relational practice between master's students and professors. *Mentoring and Tutoring: Partnership in Learning, 20*(1), 115–135.

Segal, E. (2011). Social empathy: A model built on empathy, contextual understanding, and social responsibility that promotes social justice. *Journal of Social Service Research, 37*(3), 266–277.

Seidel, S. (1998). Learning from looking. In N. Lyons (Ed.), *With portfolio in hand* (pp. 69–89). New York, NY: Teachers College Press.

Shulman, L. (2011). The scholarship of teaching and learning: A personal account and reflection. *International Journal for the Scholarship of Teaching and Learning, 5*(1), Article 30, 1–6.

Shulman, L., & Sherin, M. G. (2007). Fostering communities of teachers as learners: Disciplinary perspectives. *Journal of Curriculum Studies, 36*(2), 135–140.

Sleeter, C. E. (2008). Equity, democracy, and neoliberal assaults on teacher education. *Teaching and Teacher Education, 24*, 1947–1957.

Sleeter, C. E. (2012). Confronting the marginalization of culturally responsive pedagogy. *Urban Education, 47*(3), 562–584.

Sleeter, C. E. (2014). Toward teacher education research that informs policy. *Educational Researcher, 43*(3), 146–153.

Sowell, T. (1983). *Ethnic America: A history*. New York, NY: Basic Books.

Stevens, D. (2014). *Relational culture among staff in an emerging urban STEM high school* (Doctoral dissertation). Retrieved from rave.ohiolink.edu/etdc/view?acc_num=ucin1406880932

Stieha, V. (2010). *The relational web in teaching and learning: Connections, disconnections, and the central relational paradox in schools* (Doctoral dissertation). Retrieved from rave.ohiolink.edu/etdc/view?acc_num=ucin1276532983

Stieha, V., & Raider-Roth, M. (2011). Disrupting relationships: A catalyst for growth. In J. Faulkner (Ed.), *Disrupting pedagogies and teaching the knowledge society: Countering conservative norms with creative approaches* (pp. 16–31). Hershey, PA: Information Science Reference.

Stieha, V., & Raider-Roth, M. (2012). Presence in context: Teachers' negotiations with the relational environment of school. *Journal of Educational Change, 9*(4), 511–534.

Strieb, S., Carini, P., Kanevsky, R., & Wice, R (2011). Prospect's descriptive processes: The child, the art of teaching, and the classroom and school (Rev. ed.; 1st ed. edited by M. Himley). Prospect Archives and Center for Education and Research, North Bennington, VT. Retrieved from cdi.uvm.edu/resources/ProspectDescriptiveProcessesRevEd.pdf

Surrey, J., & Kramer, G. (2013). Relational mindfulness. In C. K. Germer, R. D. Siegel, & P. R. Fulton (Eds.), *Mindfulness and psychotherapy* (pp. 94–111). New York, NY: Guilford Press.

Tappan, M. (2001). Interpretive psychology: Stories, circles, and understanding lived experience. In D. Tolman & M. Brydon-Miller (Eds.), *From subjects to subjectivities: A handbook of interpretive and participatory methods* (pp. 45–56). New York, NY: New York University Press.

Taylor, J. M., Gilligan, C., & Sullivan, A. M. (1995). *Between voice and silence: Women and girls, race and relationship*. Cambridge, MA: Harvard University Press.

Tracy, A. J., & Sorsoli, L. (2004). A quantitative analysis method for feminist researchers: A gentle introduction (Wellesley Centers for Women working paper 414). Wellesley, MA: Wellesley Centers for Women.

Tronick, E. Z. (1989). Emotions and emotional communication in infants. *American Psychologist, 44*(2), 112–119.

Tronick, E. Z. (2007). *The neurobehavioral and social-emotional development of infants and children*. New York, NY: W. W. Norton.

Tronick, E. Z., & Weinberg, M. K. (1997). Depressed mothers and infants: Failure to form dyadic states of consciousness. In L. Murray & P. Cooper (Eds.), *Postpartum depression and child development* (pp. 54–81). New York, NY: Guilford Press.

Van Driel, J. H., & Berry, A. (2012). Teacher professional development focusing on pedagogical content knowledge. *Educational Researcher, 41*(1), 26–28.

Walker, M. (2004). How relationships heal. In M. Walker & W. B. Rosen (Eds.), *How connections heal: Stories from relational-cultural therapy* (pp. 3–21). New York, NY: Guilford Press.

Walker, M., & Miller, J. B. (2004). Racial images and relational possibilities. In J. Jordan, L. M. Hartling, & M. Walker (Eds.), *The complexity of connection: Writings from the Stone Center's Jean Baker Miller Training Institute* (pp. 129–146). New York, NY: Guilford Press.

Wei, R. C., Darling-Hammond, L., & Adamson, F. (2010). *Professional development in the United States: Trends and challenges* (Vol. 28). Dallas, TX: National Staff Development Council.

Weiser, B. (2013, November 7). Swastikas, slurs, and torment in town's schools. *New York Times*. Retrieved from nytimes.com/2013/11/08/nyregion/swastikas-slurs-and-torment-in-towns-schools.html?pagewanted=1&_r=0

Wenger, E. (1998). *Communities of practice: Learning, meaning, and identity*. Cambridge, UK: Cambridge University Press.

West, J. (2013). Deep and lifelong learning: When theory and SoTL intersect. *Journal of the Scholarship of Teaching and Learning, 13*(4), 11–20.

Whitcomb, J., Borko, H., & Liston, D. (2009). Growing talent: Promising professional development models and practices. *Journal of Teacher Education, 60*(3), 207–212.

Whitfield, S. J. (1999). *In search of American Jewish culture*. Hanover, NH: Brandeis University Press.

Whitfield, S. J. (2002). Declarations of independence: American Jewish culture in the twentieth century. In D. Biale (Ed.), *Cultures of the Jews* (Vol. 3, pp. 377–424). New York, NY: Schocken Books.

Winnicott, D. W. (1960). The theory of the parent-infant relationship. *The International Journal of Psychoanalysis, 41*, 485–495.

Zeichner, K. (2010). Competition, economic rationalization, increased surveillance, and attacks on diversity: Neo-liberalism and the transformation of teacher education in the U.S. *Teaching and Teacher Education, 26*, 1544–1552.

Index

About the Author

Miriam B. Raider-Roth is a faculty member at the University of Cincinnati, where she serves as a professor of Educational Studies and Educational/Community-Based Action Research, and was a founding director of the Center for Studies in Jewish Education and Culture. She is also the associate director of the Mandel Teacher Educator Institute. Her research focuses on the relational context of teaching and learning, action research, and feminist qualitative research methodologies. She is author of two previous books and numerous articles that examine the ways that relationships in schools shape student learning and teacher practice. Her research interests include how relational learning communities contribute to teachers' transformative learning in professional development settings.